USDA

United States
Department of
Agriculture

Forest Service

Gen. Tech. Report
WO-82b

September 2009

Forest Soil Disturbance Monitoring Protocol

Volume II: Supplementary Methods, Statistics, and Data Collection

By Deborah S. Page-Dumroese, Ann M. Abbott, and Thomas M. Rice

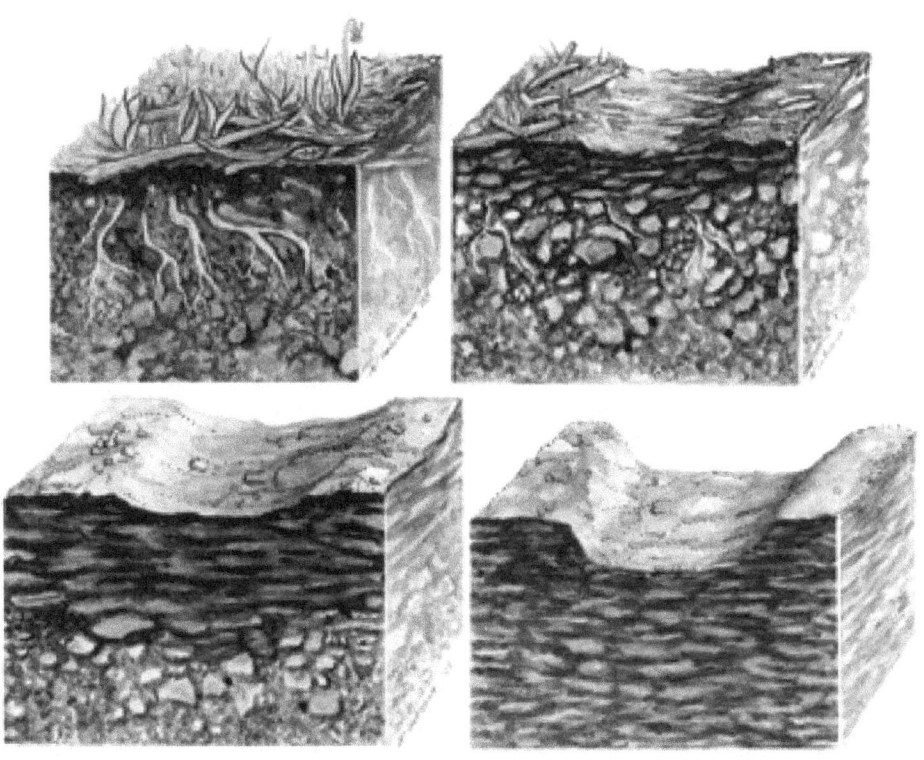

Schematics from Napper et al. (N.d.)

Contents

Acknowledgments

The monitoring approach and methods in volume I and volume II are the result of extensive collaboration between the Forest Service, U.S. Department of Agriculture National Forest System and Research and Development. The Forest Service Rocky Mountain Research Station in cooperation with the Northern Region led the effort. Although the development of this protocol has been guided by suggestions from a large number of regional soil program leaders, forest soil scientists, research soil scientists, university professors, and British Columbia Ministry of Forests and Range soil scientists, we particularly want to acknowledge the input and guidance from Sharon DeHart[1], Sue Farley[2], and Randy Davis[3]. Countless reviewers, workshop participants, students, and technicians have tested this protocol and offered input on how to make it more user friendly. Their input has been extraordinarily beneficial.

[1] Former Soil Program Leader, Northern Region, Missoula, MT.
[2] Forest Soil Scientist, Helena National Forest, Helena, MT.
[3] National Soil Program Leader, Washington Office, Washington, DC.

General Summary

This document—Volume II: Supplementary Methods, Statistics, and Data Collection—defines the science, statistical methods, and data storage components of a national Forest Soil Disturbance Monitoring Protocol. This technical guide provides the basis for a consistent method with common definitions to produce high-quality data that land managers can access and use for decisionmaking. This volume, in conjunction with Volume I: Rapid Assessment, can be used to estimate forest management effects on the soil resource. Information gathered using this protocol can easily be conveyed to and used by the general public to describe soil disturbance classes before and after management. Volume III: Scientific Background for Soil Monitoring on National Forests and Rangelands, includes state-of-the-science papers from the proceedings of a workshop.

Introduction

Volume I and volume II of the Forest Soil Disturbance Monitoring Protocol (FSDMP) provide information for a wide range of users, including technicians, field crew leaders, private landowners, land managers, forest professionals, and researchers. Volume I: Rapid Assessment includes the basic methods for establishing forest soil monitoring transects and consistently monitoring forest sites before and after ground disturbing management activities for physical attributes that could influence site resilience and long-term sustainability. Volume II: Supplementary Methods, Statistics, and Data Collection provides more details on the protocol, the historical context of forest soil monitoring, the use of statistics in forest soil monitoring, and interpretation.

Electronic Data Forms

As we improve the protocol, we periodically update the electronic data forms, which users can download from http://forest.moscowfsl.wsu.edu/smp/solo/documents/monitoring/forms/.

A database is being developed for storage of data collected using the FSDMP. Data recorded on the electronic field forms will be converted to database format and imported into the national FSDMP database when it becomes available. In the interim, the data should be kept locally and/or on regional servers.

Initially, the national FSDMP database will combine the features of two existing products—the Forest Service Rocky Mountain Research Station and the Northern Region SoLo database and Southern Region ONSITE disturbance calculator—and will ultimately be linked to or integrated with the Natural Resource Information System.

SoLo is an online report filing system on the Northern Region computer system. It is accessible only on the Forest Service secure intranet (fsweb) and features user profile management, a secure login, keyword search capability, a data input interface, and data summary and export functions. The input interface is in seven parts: site identification, site location, site characteristics, site history, current activity and effects, summary/ conclusions, and administrative information.

ONSITE is a Microsoft® Access® database that is distributable on compact disc (CD) in either a user or an administrator version. It is designed for recording large areas of disturbance in an activity area. Within the database are forms to record site identification, location, physical characteristics, and soil disturbance types (loss/movement, alteration, fire) by area affected, plus a "Tally Sheet" that will calculate area based on the shape of the disturbance (circle, oval, rectangle, or triangle).

Historical Context for Monitoring Forest Soils

Although many definitions describe what soil quality is, or should be, on public lands in the United States, maintenance of soil productive capacity is a common objective. Maintaining soil productivity and quality on National Forest System land is governed by the Multiple Use and Sustained Yield Act of 1969, the Forest and Rangeland Renewable Resources Planning Act of 1974, and the National Forest Management Act (NFMA) of 1976. The important role of soil productivity to sustainable forestry is clear, but which soil properties to monitor as indicators of forest sustainability are not so clear (Burger and Kelting 1998, Page-Dumroese et al. 2000, Staddon et al. 1999).

The challenge has been the development of meaningful soil quality standards to evaluate the full range of variability found in forest soils (Page-Dumroese et al. 2000). Many forest soils are resilient to management activities (e.g., timber harvests, hazardous fuel reductions, prescribed fire, and site preparation), while others are at risk of losing the productive capacity after vegetation management because of limitations in the inherent soil properties (e.g., shallow forest floor or thin mineral mantles over bedrock [Burger and Kelting 1999]). Therefore, establishing monitoring variables and protocols that are practical to use, give meaningful information over a wide range of sites, and provide a benchmark for evaluating soil change is critical (Page-Dumroese et al. 2000). Adequate baseline assessments of important site-specific properties such as forest floor depth, soil cover, and so on will help make accurate and realistic projections of potential site changes from management activities. NFMA (and related legislation) required the United States Secretary of Agriculture to ensure, through research and monitoring, that the national forests be managed to protect the permanent productivity of the land (USDA Forest Service 1983). The Forest Service established the first approximation of working soil quality standards throughout the Federal regions (Page-Dumroese et al. 2000, Powers et al. 1998). The first approximation standards were meant as monitoring tools that were presumed to reflect site potential and to mark thresholds for significantly impaired productivity.

The Forest Service program of the North American Long-Term Soil Productivity (LTSP) program was built on the principle that, within the constraints of climate, a site's productive capacity is governed strongly by physical, chemical, and biological processes affected readily by management. The fundamental properties of soil porosity and site organic matter govern a site's response to management by their roles in water and gas exchange, rooting restrictions, microbial activity, soil aggregate stability, and overall resource availability (Powers et al. 2005). These LTSP sites are now 15 years old and are beginning to reach crown closure. Numerous research papers have been published (e.g., Busse et al. 2006; Fleming et al. 2006; Page-Dumroese et al. 2006a; Sanchez et al.

2006) detailing changes in site processes and tree growth. The LTSP study provides the calibrations to link the soil disturbances described within this document with changes in potential productivity.

Soil Disturbance

Soil quality is a moving target and our ideas of what it is and how to measure it have evolved over the years. Unfortunately, it cannot be measured directly (Powers et al. 1998). The conundrum is to define the functional elements of soil that sustain biological productivity and to identify soil quality indicators of these functions (Powers et al. 1998). Useful indicators must be sensitive to variations in climate and management; integrate soil physical, chemical, and biological properties; and be practical and useable by a variety of disciplines. Therefore, defining the functional elements of soil that sustain biological productivity and identifying indicators of those properties are key to the success of monitoring. Useful indicators have been proposed for agricultural systems that have less spatial variability and more management intensity (Doran and Parkin 1994, Larson and Pierce 1994, Warkentin 1995) than are commonly found in forest soils (Burger and Kelting 1998). Because the processes and properties of forest soils are more varied and less well understood, a detailed, intensive approach (Doran and Parkin 1994) is probably not justified for monitoring forest soil quality extensively in the United States (Burger and Kelting 1998, Powers et al. 1998).

Soil disturbance in forested ecosystems most commonly occurs from ground-based harvest and site preparation (mechanical and fire) activities, but it can also occur as sheet or rill erosion. After a review of the apparent evidence that soil productivity has declined under forest management (Morris and Miller 1994, Powers et al. 1990), changes in soil physical properties and organic matter content were noted as two factors that could alter soil quality, by changing the ability of roots to support leaf mass and primary productivity (Powers et al. 1998).

The effects of soil disturbance on soil productivity, soil quality, or site hydrologic function are dependent on the *degree, extent, distribution,* and *duration* of the effects (Clayton et al. 1987, Craigg and Howes 2007, Froehlich 1976, Snider and Miller 1985).

The degree and duration of soil disturbance effects are largely determined by inherent soil properties, such as texture, coarse-fragment content, or organic matter content. Extent, distribution, and, in some instances, degree of soil disturbance can be controlled by management constraints, such as changing the season of operation, spacing of skid roads, or the number of equipment passes.

Soil Disturbance Effects on Productivity Are Determined by...

Degree refers to the amount of change in any one particular property (bulk density, porosity, etc.) and the depth of change into the soil profile.

Extent refers to the amount of land surface affected by the disturbance (usually expressed as a percentage).

Distribution of soil disturbance within a management area can either be relatively evenly dispersed throughout the unit in small polygons or be concentrated in one (or more) larger feature(s).

Duration is the length of time disturbance effects persist.

To monitor and quantify changes in soil properties that could have potentially detrimental effects on site productivity or hydrologic function, we need a consistent method to assess and report soil disturbance that occurs as a result of management activities. Simply stating that a single threshold beyond which detrimental soil conditions are thought to exist is neither practical nor desirable (Craigg and Howes 2007). Forest managers do not wish to degrade soil productivity or cause impaired watershed function, and they should not be unnecessarily limited in management opportunities (Craigg and Howes 2007). The soil disturbance classification system described in this volume provides technical direction to enable effective communication of results to specialists and the public. It also provides for a comparison of operational results from one site to another.

Our objectives for this volume are to recommend common terms for describing forest soil disturbance, detail a statistically sound technique for applying visual classes for routine forest soil monitoring, and provide reliable methods for classifying the effects of management.

Why Use Visual Classes?

Forest management activities all have the potential to create soil disturbances. Some soil disturbance may be beneficial if it is planned and conducted under suitable soil conditions by the proper equipment. The removal of forest floor material, displacement of the mineral soil, compaction, puddling, erosion, and high burn severity, however, can have potentially negative effects on site productivity and hydrologic responses. The Forest Service must be able to manage soil disturbance in order to maintain sustainable production of natural resources (Craigg and Howes 2007).

Describing or defining soil disturbance in terms of variables such as soil strength, pore space, or bulk density makes assessing soil changes resulting from management activities difficult and expensive. Soil variability and variation in the pattern of equipment operations or burning activities further complicates assessments. Other factors such as climate (both macro- and micro-), vegetation management practices, genetics, and distribution of hazardous fuels can affect the *extent* and *degree* of soil disturbance and subsequent effects on site productivity. In addition, several forms of disturbance can occur in one location, adding to the complexity of the assessments. For example, forest floor removal, mineral soil displacement, and compaction often occur in the same location. In most forest soils, bulk density (the measure of compaction) increases with increasing depth. In soils where the topsoil has been displaced, the natural increase in bulk density could be confused with compaction.

One way to simplify and standardize soil disturbance assessments is to use visual classes to describe the degree of change from natural or preactivity conditions to those resulting from management activities. Soil disturbance visual classes also enable soil scientists to more easily communicate desired soil conditions and display effects to members of the public, contract administrators, and other resource specialists. Soil disturbance occurs in a continuum over the landscape and the visual disturbance class method enables an observer to divide the continuum into meaningful, describable, repeatable segments. Regardless of which soil indicators are ultimately selected, they should be comparable to an available baseline, be timely, be applicable over a large area, and be inexpensive and easy to use (Burger and Kelting 1999). They should also provide an effective means for communicating the effects of land management on soil resilience and productivity.

Visual classes have been used by a variety of public and private entities (e.g., Block et al. 2002, Craigg and Howes 2007, Curran et al. 2005, Heninger et al. 2002, Page-Dumroese et al. 2006b) for the assessment of change in soil disturbance from preactivity to post-activity. Visual classes offer a method to efficiently and consistently gather information about soil disturbance. Curran et al. (2007) report that visual disturbance categories provide a practical method for describing soil disturbances in a forested setting. Several soil scientists in the western United States (e.g., Craigg and Howes 2007, Curran et al. 2005, Curran et al. 2007, Heninger et al. 2002, Howes et al. 1983, Page-Dumroese et al. 2006b) have conducted research on using visual indicators. The previous authors of visual indicator research provide additional background information on the visual indicators used in the FSDMP (table 1). Selection of these indicators is based on several field seasons of research and testing across the forested United States and collaborative work with the British Columbia Ministry of Forests and Range and published literature.

Table 1.—*Visual indicators and their definitions.*

Forest floor impacted	Forest floor material includes all organic horizons above the mineral soil surface.
Topsoil displacement	The surface mineral soil primarily includes the A horizons, but if the A horizon is shallow or undeveloped, it may include other horizons. This disturbance is usually due to machinery but does not include "rutting" described below.
Rutting	Ruts vary in depth but are primarily the result of equipment movement. Ruts are defined as machine-generated soil displacement or compression. Often soil puddling is also present within the rut.
Burning (light, moderate, severe)	Burn severity includes only effects on the forest floor and mineral soil, not on above-ground vegetation.
Compaction	Compaction by equipment results in either a compression of the soil profile or increased resistance to penetration.
Platy structure/ massive/puddled	Platy or tabular structure in the mineral soil. Massive soil indicates no structural units are present and soil material is a coherent mass. Puddled soil is often found after wet weather harvest operations. Soil pores are usually smeared and prevent water infiltration.

In this FSDMP, disturbance classes (table 2) are used as a proxy to determine whether observed soil disturbances could be considered detrimental to soil productivity or hydrologic function. Ideally, validation of vegetative response or changes in hydrologic function will occur for various soil types, logging practices, and forest types. After a soil disturbance class is determined at each sample point within an activity area, the information can then be aggregated to calculate how much detrimental soil disturbance exists in an activity area and what the amount and distribution of detrimental soil disturbance could mean for long-term productivity.

Table 2.—*Soil disturbance classes used in the Forest Soil Disturbance Monitoring Protocol. Soil disturbance classes increase in severity of impact from class 0 to class 3.*

Soil disturbance class 0	Soil disturbance class 1
Soil surface: • No evidence of compaction; i.e., past equipment operation, ruts, skid trails. • No depressions or wheel tracks evident. • Forest floor layers present and intact. • No soil displacement evident. • No management-generated soil erosion. • Litter and duff layers not burned. No soil char. Water repellency may be present.	Soil surface: • Faint wheel tracks or slight depressions evident and are <5 cm deep. • Forest floor layers present and intact. • Surface soil has not been displaced and shows minimal mixing with subsoil. • Burning light: Depth of char <1 cm. ***Accessory*:*** Litter charred or consumed. Duff largely intact. Water repellency is similar to preburn conditions. Soil compaction: • Compaction in the surface soil is slightly greater than observed under natural conditions. • Concentrated from 0 to 10 cm deep. Observations of soil physical conditions: • Change in soil structure from crumb or granular structure to massive or platy structure; restricted to the surface, 0 to 10 cm. • Platy structure is noncontinuous. • Fine, medium, and large roots can penetrate or grow around the platy structure. No "J" rooting observed. • Erosion is slight.
Soil disturbance class 2	**Soil disturbance class 3**
Soil surface: • Wheel tracks or depressions are 5 to 10 cm deep. • ***Accessory*:*** Forest floor layers partially intact or missing. • Surface soil partially intact and may be mixed with subsoil. • Burning moderate: Depth of char is 1 to 5 cm. Accessory*: Duff deeply charred or consumed. Surface-soil water repellency increased compared with the preburn condition. Soil compaction: • Increased compaction is present from 10 to 30 cm deep. Observation of soil physical condition: • Change in soil structure from crumb or granular structure to massive or platy structure; restricted to the surface, 10 to 30 cm. • Platy structure is generally continuous. • ***Accessory*:*** Large roots may penetrate the platy structure, but fine and medium roots may not. • Erosion is moderate.	Soil surface: • Wheel tracks and depressions highly evident with depth >10 cm. • ***Accessory*:*** Forest floor layers missing. • Evidence of surface soil removal, gouging, and piling. • Most surface soil displaced. Surface soil may be mixed with subsoil. Subsoil partially or totally exposed. • Burning severe: Depth of char is >5 cm. ***Accessory*:*** Duff and litter layer completely consumed. Surface soil is water repellent. Surface is reddish or orange in places. Soil compaction: • Increased compaction is deep in the soil profile (>30 cm deep). Observations of soil physical conditions: • Change in soil structure from granular structure to massive or platy structure extends beyond 30 cm deep. • Platy structure is continuous. • ***Accessory*:*** Roots do not penetrate the platy structure. • Erosion is severe and has produced deep gullies or rills.

* *Accessory items are those descriptors that may help identify individual severity classes.*

Current Forest Soil Needs

The FSDMP was developed in response to a growing need for a common understanding of soil disturbance monitoring in forested settings. The protocol is designed to meet a wide range of needs, including project-level implementation or effects monitoring. The FSDMP is a rapid assessment tool that is easy to implement and is usable at different scales and intensities. In addition, because it is used in a consistent manner, data can be aggregated. The FSDMP was developed to address vegetation management effects to soil quality in forested ecosystems. Other monitoring protocols, such as the *Monitoring Manual for Grassland, Shrubland, and Savanna Ecosystems* (Herrick et al. 2005), are more appropriate for assessing the effects of management to soils supporting shrubland and grassland ecosystems.

Key Concepts

The FSDMP is meant to be a rapid assessment of preactivity and postactivity soil disturbance that provides a consistent and repeatable method to describe visual physical soil indicators. It is intended for use by field soil scientists and watershed specialists, with broad application for other disciplines. Field soil scientists and managers can predetermine the types of information they need as they plan activities that cause soil disturbance and the subsequent need for monitoring projects. This protocol also offers an opportunity to consider what kinds of decisions will need to be made, how information will be used, what need exists for highly precise information (risk), and how much the monitoring effort will cost (Howes 2006).

For use in forested settings, this monitoring protocol assesses soil surface disturbance. The protocol can be used to monitor preactivity and postactivity area disturbance and was designed to be flexible enough to be used following a variety of forest management practices on the full range of soil types. Some changes (such as compaction and rutting), however, are linked to an increase in that property at depth. Numerous equipment trips or deep ruts are often evidence of deep soil compaction, but not always. A shovel or metal probe may be needed to determine the actual depth of compaction.

Sampling protocols similar to this have been used in Forest Service Regions 1 and 6 for both research and operational studies. They have been used to monitor the effects of soil compaction on initial height growth of ponderosa pine (Cochran and Brock 1985), the effect of feller-bunchers on soil disturbance (Laing and Howes 1988), and the effect of tractor yarding and machine piling on 24 timber sales (Sullivan 1987) and to determine the effects of wildfire and salvage logging on soil disturbance on all the national forests

> **Rapid Assessment**
>
> The FSDMP provides for a variety of alternatives to suit the monitoring objective. You can—
>
> 1. Vary the *intensity* of sampling by changing the confidence level,
>
> 2. Vary the *number* of soil attributes used for calculating sample size, and/or
>
> 3. Use *ONSITE* to calculate the areal extent of large features.

in the Forest Service Northern Region (Page-Dumroese et al. 2006b). In addition, similar visual class systems are being used in British Columbia (Curran et al. 2005) and Saskatchewan (Block et al. 2002). Information gathered from these monitoring efforts can be used to adjust harvest and site preparation practices (Howes 2006).

Because the results of management activities on soil productivity vary by soil type (Fleming et al. 2006, Gomez et al. 2002, Page-Dumroese et al. 2000, Page-Dumroese et al. 2006b, Powers et al. 2005), this document does not prescribe any disturbance class as detrimental disturbance. The FSDMP establishes a standard inventory, monitoring, and assessment tool. In addition, it provides common terms. Storing data in the SoLo database (see appendix C for a description of the FSDMPSoLo monitoring worksheets) will allow for consistent data interpretation at local, regional, and national levels and will facilitate data sharing. Monitoring results can also help determine if current Forest Service Regional Soil Quality Standards are being met.

Relationship to Other Federal Inventory and Monitoring Programs

This volume of the FSDMP presents a protocol for field measurement of physical soil disturbance. The protocol is for site-specific analysis of management-induced soil disturbance in an activity area (e.g., a harvest unit or prescribed burn). This protocol differs from other Forest Service or other Federal agency monitoring programs because it is designed to collect site-specific data at the project level.

Programs in Other Federal Agencies

The Natural Resource Conservation Service (NRCS) leads the national soil survey program. This program is a mid-scale soil mapping and characterization project that informs field soil scientists as they plan their workload for site-specific forest management projects. Nationwide, many national forests have or are working toward having a soil survey completed for the forest, excluding wilderness areas.

Changes to the Current Protocol (Change Management)

Volumes I and II, which detail the FSDMP, are dynamic documents; changes to the outlined protocol are inevitable as sites are monitored and data are analyzed. Changes to the protocol must be carefully considered, however, so that the objective of having a consistent approach to obtaining physical soil data is met. New science related to soil monitoring or management effects may initiate a review and suggest changes to this protocol. Changes to the FSDMP can also be initiated from the field, but they must be subject to peer and research review. In addition, collaborations with industry, private, tribal, and international land management organizations could lead to the development of other soil disturbance monitoring and conservation procedures. These collaborations will allow for continuous evolution of best management practices, enable coordinated development of training and tools, facilitate reporting, and enhance the exchange of research results (Curran et al. 2005).

Determining the Type of Transect To Use

Transects can be positioned in a variety of ways within the activity area. Three examples are outlined in appendix A.

Stratifying an Activity Area

As outlined in volume I, many monitoring strategies are available. Because of site variability, it can be useful in some cases to stratify an activity area to increase monitoring efficiency and to provide better estimators when there are discrete areas of homogeneous disturbance. For example, disturbance may be confined to one area or it could be dispersed across the entire activity area. Stratifying an activity area may help improve both the accuracy and precision by finding the most efficient monitoring polygons. Monitoring efficiency is defined as resulting in lower variability estimates than would have been achieved without stratification.

If the Unit Is Large

It may not be feasible to monitor a large activity area (100 ha (~250 acres or more) in its entirety. As noted in the following text, however, a large area can be stratified into more discrete units to make monitoring more efficient. Use the following options as a guide to help determine the most appropriate monitoring strategy.

- Complete a rapid assessment of the entire activity area and take a *minimum* of 30 sample points. This option is recommended if the activity area is uniform relative to the soils, vegetation, slope, and aspect.

- If the activity area is not uniform ecologically or in terms of disturbance (e.g., different habitat types, sensitive soils, log decks, skid trails), it is recommended to stratify the sample. Stratification will allow for detailed monitoring on areas that have had previous entry; have mechanical, ground-based equipment off system roads; or are ecologically sensitive. As long as the point samples are collected at random or systematically (see appendix A for options on how to lay out sample points) and are based on the established protocols, the statistics of this subsample will be valid. The key is to document what was monitored and why.

Activity areas may not need a large number of sample points if the amount of variability is low. The number of monitoring points needed depends only on the variability within the activity area and not on its size. Validation monitoring completed in the Northern Region suggests that sample points spaced ~20 m (~65 ft) apart were close enough to determine the variability within activity areas that were ~50 ha (~125 acres) in size (Page-Dumroese et al. 2006b).

The Number of Activity Areas To Monitor

It is important to consider how the data are going to be used, what the soil disturbance risk is, and what the variability of the individual activity area and analysis area are when determining how many areas to monitor. Use the FSDMP on enough activity areas within an analysis area so it is possible to interpret ratings for existing and detrimental disturbance and for mitigations, monitoring, or restoration prescriptions. If past monitoring or research demonstrates that similar activities, under similar climatic conditions and management, have resulted in disturbance levels well within the accepted maximum, then it is sufficient to visit the site and confirm that this is a typical activity area.

Unique Monitoring Strategies

Monitoring points may fall on unusual features such as on large boulders, in down wood, under fallen trees or "tip-ups," on stumps, within bushes, and in stream beds. If such monitoring points occur, you can offset a small distance from the transect line. Plan before you leave the office for what rules you will use to offset from unusual features. For instance, you may want to decide that offsetting 1 m (3 ft) west from any feature is appropriate, or you may decide that if a point falls on an unusual feature, it will be listed as "did not count." Because the FSDMP assesses soil surface condition, it is important to note what the soil surface is. If you cannot assess the disturbance at or near a point because of obstacles (rocks, downed wood, stumps, etc.), record the presence of the obstacle(s), but then indicate "did not count" in the comment field and exclude that point from the data analysis by entering a period (.) in the cell for each indicator. Do not record either a "1" (present) or a "0" (absent) for any indicator at that point and do not leave a blank space. Keep in mind, however, that on some sites it is "normal" to have a larger number of surface rocks. If this condition is the case, a monitoring point falling on this feature should be counted.

Wildfire

Wildfires are not assessed with this protocol. This protocol is designed to describe land management activity effects to the soil resource.

Prescribed Fire or Burn Piles

The effect of these management activities is considered in the FSDMP. These types of burns may or may not be detrimental to subsequent vegetative growth. Guidelines for assessing prescribed burn intensity are contained in the disturbance class definitions (table 3).

Table 3.—*Examples of soil visual indicators and management activities. (1 of 2)*

Disturbance type	Severity class			
	0	1	2	3
Equipment impacts				
Past operation	None.	Dispersed.	Faint.	Obvious.
Wheel tracks or depressions	None.	Faint wheel tracks or slight depressions evident (<5 cm deep).	Wheel tracks or depressions are >5 cm deep.	Wheel tracks or depressions highly evident with a depth being >10 cm.

Disturbance type	Severity class			
	0	1	2	3
Equipment trails from more than two passes	None.	Faintly evident.	Evident, but not heavily trafficked.	Main trails that are heavily used.
Excavated and bladed trails[1]	None.	None.	None.	Present.
Penetration and resistance[2]	Natural conditions.	Resistance of surface soils may be slightly greater than observed under natural conditions. Increased resistance is concentrated in the surface (10 cm).	Increased resistance is present throughout the top 30 cm of soil.	Increased resistance is deep into the soil profile (>30 cm).
Soil structure	Natural conditions.	Change in soil structure from crumb or granular structure to massive or platy structure in the surface (10 cm).	Change in soil structure in the surface (30 cm). Platy (or massive) structure is generally continuous. On older sites, large roots may penetrate the platy structure, but fine and medium roots may not.	Change in soil structure extends beyond the top 30 cm. Platy (or massive) structure is continuous. On older sites, roots do not penetrate the platy structure.
Displacement				
Forest floor	None.	Forest floor layers present and intact.	Forest floor layers partially intact or missing.	Forest floor layers missing.
Mineral soil	None.	Soil surface has not been displaced and shows minimal mixing with subsoil.	Mineral topsoil partially intact and may be mixed with subsoil.	Evidence of topsoil removal, gouging, and piling. Soil displacement has removed most of the surface soil. Surface soil may be mixed with subsoil or subsoil may be partially or totally exposed.
Erosion	None.	Slight erosion evident (i.e., sheet erosion[3]).	Moderate amount of erosion evident (i.e., sheet and rill erosion[3]).	Substantial amount of erosion evident. Gullies, pedestals, and rills noticeable.
Burning	None.	Fire impacts are light. Forest floor is charred but intact. Gray ash becomes inconspicuous and surface appears lightly charred to black. Soil surface structure intact.	Fire impacts are moderate. Litter layer is consumed and humus layer is charred or consumed. Mineral soil not visibly altered, but soil organic matter (OM) has been partially charred.	Fire impacts are deep. The entire forest floor is consumed and top layer of mineral soil is visibly altered. Surface mineral structure and texture are altered. Mineral soil is black due to charred or deposited OM or is orange from burning.

[1] *Evaluate on main trails but not necessarily for wheel tracks or depressions.*

[2] *Soil resistance to penetration with a tile spade or probe is best done when the soil is not moist or wet.*

[3] *USDA NRCS (1993).*

Unburned Slash Piles

Unburned or partially burned slash piles can be found on former landings, on skid roads, or in the previously harvested activity area. When these features are on landings or skid roads, they should be assessed as part of those structures because the underlying soil will probably be similar to the surrounding affected area. Similarly, if an old slash pile is located in the harvest activity area, it is likely that the soil beneath the pile could be affected to the same degree as the surrounding soil. It is often difficult to examine the soil beneath some slash piles, however, so if an inference is made about the soil beneath the slash pile from the surrounding soil, a note should be made in the comments. If a confident prediction cannot be made about the soil under a slash pile, then indicate "did not count" on the *Data entry* worksheet (see appendix C-3).

Landings, Temporary Roads, and System Roads

System roads generally are not included in the activity area. System roads are part of the permanent transportation system and the land has been removed from the productive land base.

- Landings and temporary roads that are outside the activity area are not included. Landings and temporary roads usually limit vegetative growth by their very nature. If desired during monitoring, an acreage (length times average width based on a traverse study, aerial photo, or ONSITE worksheet) of these features can be kept if needed for existing condition, project effects, and cumulative effects discussions.

- Landings and temporary roads that are inside the activity area are counted and contribute to the amount of disturbance within an activity area. In addition to recording the disturbance class of these features, acreage (length times average width based on a traverse study, aerial photo, or similar method) of these features can be recorded to describe the existing condition, project effects, and cumulative effects.

Root Ball or Bole of a "Tip-Up"

If a monitoring point lands on the root ball or bole of a fallen tree, it is counted as coarse wood with a remark in the comment section stating "roots of fallen tree" or "tip-up." If the reason for the tree tip can be determined, it should be noted. If the tree tip can be associated to human activity and a monitoring point falls on it, then that point is assigned a disturbance class based on what is observed immediately adjacent to the monitoring point. If the tree tip is not associated with human activity, the monitoring point is assigned class 0.

Spreadsheet Forms

Examples of the four electronic worksheets used for the FSDMP are shown in appendix C (*SoLo Info, Variable Selection, Data Entry, Results*) and we provide an *Attachment* worksheet for uploading maps, photos, or other important site information (form not shown). As we endeavor to improve these methods, these worksheets may change. Check the following Web site for the most recent version before starting work in the field: http://forest. moscowfsl.wsu.edu/smp/solo/InfoPath/monitoring/documents.php (look in the "FORMS" section). The worksheets were designed so forest soil monitoring consistently evaluates a standard set of soil disturbance indicators; this is the rationale behind having to fill out each column completely before moving on to the next monitoring point. Do not modify the field form; the field form was also designed to make data entry into the electronic database quick and easy. Storing the data in an electronic database is part of the FSDMP.

Paper Field Form

Field data can be collected on paper field forms and then transferred into the electronic spreadsheet. Do not modify any of the worksheets within the spreadsheet as they will directly link to the electronic database. You can select the soil attributes you need, but do not change any of the fields. All data collected, whether on paper or electronic forms, should be entered into the FSDMPSoLo database.

When using the paper field form, use the sample size table (see appendix D for both the paper field form and the sample size tables) must also be used. Users should stop at the end of the first 30 monitoring points and calculate the proportion of disturbed points within the first 30 by adding the number of "1s" entered and then dividing by 30 (see appendix B for the statistics behind the FSDMP). This proportion is $\hat{p}$ and should be entered in the column labeled visual class proportions. The visual class proportion must then be located in the sample size table along with the associated sample size. Determining the sample size can be done for each indicator variable in the *Data Entry* form (see appendix C-3) or for the indicator that is the primary concern. Of primary interest are the most commonly occurring indicators. After the sample size is determined for each indicator variable, the largest sample size from the list of monitoring attributes should be used for the activity area sample size. An exception to this rule could occur if a single indicator variable is more variable than all the others, resulting in one sample size being much greater than all the rest (where "much greater" is defined as being more than 1.5 times the sample size of the next lower sample size) and the professional judgment of the observer is such that the indicator variable in question is not representative of the activity area and/

or a concern on that soil type. In this case, the next lower sample size should be selected and a thorough explanation must be made in the comments.

It should be noted that the sample sizes calculated from the first 30 points are likely to be different from those calculated from a greater number; varying the intensity of the sample (lowering the confidence interval) may reduce the total number of sample points needed. The observer is free to choose some number higher than 30 for the first set, which may be more efficient if it initially appears that the soil disturbance within an activity is highly variable. The observer can also recalculate the sample size a second time if the initial sample size is quite large.

Portable Data Recorder and Electronic Field Form

It is recommended that all data be entered into an electronic database that is searchable by any ecological state, location, characteristic, or activity. To use the electronic *Data Entry* worksheet (see appendix C-3) in a portable data recorder (PDR) (see appendix F), the user must enter the confidence level. Although the full range of confidence levels is available (from 70 percent to 90 percent), each site should be assessed individually to select the best one. All columns for data entry must be filled in. Do not leave blanks within the form, or the sample sizes and confidence intervals will be incorrect. We recommend filling out the columns for each sample point as the point is actually observed. If a point is not observable, fill in the column for that point with periods (.) and document the reason why the point "did not count" (see the Unique Monitoring Strategies section for definitions). DO NOT FILL IN THESE POINTS WITH ZEROS.

The electronic spreadsheet (on the *Data Entry* worksheet; see appendix C-3) calculates sample size and confidence intervals automatically and updates each additional monitoring point (on the *Results* worksheet; see appendix C-4); however, until the first 30 monitoring points are entered, the values for sample size are preset to 30 and confidence intervals are invalid. It is important to note that if the worksheet is prefilled with zeros, the sample sizes and confidence intervals are likely to reflect an inaccurately low level of variability and are likely to be incorrect.

The required sample size shown on the electronic spreadsheet is the largest of the sample sizes calculated for the individual indicator variables. The individual sample sizes can be seen by changing to the *Results* worksheet (see appendix C-4). If the required sample is more than 1.5 times larger than the next lower sample size and the professional judgment of the observer is that the indicator variable is an anomaly within the activity area, the next lower sample size can be chosen and a thorough explanation made in the comments.

Field Data Collection—Standards and Methods

The core soil disturbance indicators (table 1) should be collected at each monitoring point, but the user has the ability to "turn off" soil indicators (changing the *number* of indicators) that do not pertain to the project area being monitored (see *Variable Selection* worksheet, appendix C-2). After the soil indicator data have been collected, additional data can also be collected using other published protocols (e.g., bulk density or soil hydrophobicity). When using other protocols, document what they are and on which sites they were used.

Filling in the Worksheets

Data To Collect in the Office

Before beginning a field evaluation of soil disturbance on an activity area, available existing information sources should be studied and applicable information should be recorded the *SoLo Info* worksheet (see appendix C-1) and additional information on these site descriptors can be found in appendix G. Time spent in the office gathering information before field sampling and determining the kind of transect, the number of points, and the indicators needed can reduce field time and monitoring costs.

In general, the following steps should be followed before going in the field:

1. Consult the most current subsection map (McNab et al. 2007) and available landtype association maps for general site characteristics. The SoLo database may require some of this information, which can help stratify the area for sampling. It is important to note, however, that such broad-scale maps are not appropriate for the more detailed site information needed to assess soil quality.

2. Consult available soil surveys and terrestrial ecological unit inventories (TEUIs) for more detailed site information and for the description and morphology of the soils that occur in the project area. Soil surveys may have been done by the Forest Service or by the Natural Resources Conservation Service (NRCS) and may be referred to as soil resource inventories, TEUIs, or landtype inventories. This information can help establish soil reference conditions for the activity area. It is critical, however, to confirm the actual soil type after you are in the field.

3. Check previous field review and soil monitoring reports and use available data.

4. For postactivity assessments, consult the harvest plan and contract information to determine where existing skid trails, landings, or changes in harvest operations may have occurred.

Selecting Indicators

The indicators in the *Variable Selection* spreadsheet (see appendix C-2) are those that most closely align soil quality standards, data from research studies, and previous visual guide information. You may want to use some or all of these for preactivity and postactivity monitoring. After the monitoring objective has been set (see the following section), select the indicators, the transect configuration, and the confidence levels to meet those objectives.

Some monitoring considerations include the timing of postactivity monitoring. Monitoring an activity area within 1 year of completion will provide answers related to the harvest or postharvest activities. Monitoring an activity area 3 to 5 years after completion will provide an indication of how resilient the soils are and the short-term duration of the disturbance. Some disturbance, however, will be much less visible after 1 to 2 years, particularly small-scale features in areas where litterfall is significant. Longer term monitoring is often not feasible in this context and studies such as *The North American Long-Term Soil Productivity Experiment: Findings From the First Decade of Research* (Powers et al. 2005) will provide answers to long-term effects of soil disturbance on vegetative growth.

Monitoring Objectives

For monitoring to achieve the goal of detecting change, it must be performed both before and after an activity. Each of these events, within the context of a rapid assessment, serves a different purpose. If field time is limited, using the FSDMP in conjunction with ONSITE (areal extent of large features) can help get the most relevant information that can be transferred to similar sites. Data that are collected in the same way and that use the same indicators ensure that you can match data and sites.

Using a *preactivity assessment* will provide a baseline or reference condition against which change or disturbance can be measured. On sites known to be undisturbed—that is, have never been affected by human enterprise—only minimal assessment may be necessary. On these undisturbed sites, simply fill out the form in appendix E.

On sites known to be previously disturbed, a low-intensity rapid assessment can be used to reveal the location and extent of a previous disturbance, which will be useful in planning and estimating cumulative effects. Information can be gleaned from previous project reports and stand histories, and, depending on the variability seen on these sites, a formal 30-point-minimum assessment using the FSDMP may be recommended.

Step-by-Step Field Survey Method

The steps to follow for a *Rapid Assessment* are explained in Vol. I.; the key information and steps are also listed here. For the FSDMP, the monitoring point of soil surface disturbance is taken in a 15-cm (6-in) diameter circular area (a "toe-point" assessment). By using the sample size calculator and appropriate confidence level, the project area can be adequately assessed using the circular point for disturbance classes. The visual disturbance category is chosen by selecting the one best fitting the monitoring point.

As the activity area is walked, each monitoring point along the transect or at each grid point is placed in one of the predefined classes (table 3). The monitoring point may represent soil attributes from more than one classification, and the soil scientist or other observer may have to make a decision about which visual disturbance class best describes the sample point. This protocol is to be used where activity areas are defined and discrete. For assessment of areas in a watershed context, without defined and discrete units, see the section titled "Unique Monitoring Strategies."

Baseline (Preactivity) Assessment

Step 1. Prework—Determine why you are monitoring (goals) and if the FSDMP is the most efficient method for accomplishing those goals. As noted in the section titled "Data To Collect While in the Office," fill out as much of the electronic or paper form as possible using existing documentation and interviews with other team members (see also appendix G). Inspection of topographic maps and areal photography can reveal basic landform information, such as slope and drainage patterns that affect soil productivity or hydrologic function. Select the variables you want to use for monitoring the activity area (see the *Variable Selection* worksheet, appendix C-2). Determine the size of the activity area. Determine which option for monitoring point layout will work best for your site (see appendix A). If choosing a random transect, select the length of transect needed and the distance between points. If choosing a grid point survey, select a random orientation for the grid points. If using an electronic PDR, predetermine grid point locations and save them onto the recorder.

Step 2. Select the *Data Entry* worksheet (see appendix C-3). If past ground-disturbing activities (e.g., stumps, skid trails, roads, differences in vegetation age or composition, or trash) are evident, continue to use the FSDMP for a quantitative estimate of the amount and extent of disturbance. Often, aerial photos and other maps can be used to determine the extent of effects. Field verification of compaction, displacement, or change in hydrologic state is necessary on sites with legacy effects. From preactivity assessments, determination of cumulative effects may be facilitated. Conversely, if records of previous management resulted in minimal soil disturbance and the activity area has similar soils, vegetation, aspect, and slope throughout the unit, then space a *minimum* of 30 monitoring points to cover the entire unit. When using the sample size calculator and appropriate confidence level, more points may be necessary. Take note of preactivity forest floor depth and composition, mineral soil horizon depth(s), and depth to bedrock (if applicable).

Step 3. Document a preactivity starting point using a Global Positioning System or other method of precise point location documentation. Using the sampling scheme selected from step 1, start sampling 5 m (~15 ft) inside the unit to avoid edge effects. If using a PDR (see appendix F), upload a map of the site and add predetermined monitoring point locations before going into the field. Predetermining monitoring point locations can also be done with paper copies of available maps.

Step 4. After locating the starting point within the activity area, calculate the distance between points based on activity area size. To avoid bias, sample point distances must be predetermined and documented before starting. Points must be evenly spaced to cover the entire activity area. For instance, if the activity area is ~1,000 m (3,300 ft) long and you need to take 30 sample points, points should be at least 35 m (110 ft) apart along the random transect. If the transect (or point grid) does not adequately cover the range of variability, then take more transects (or grid points) to confirm the presence or absence of dispersed disturbance and the nature of the dispersed disturbance.

Step 5. Walk to the first point and assess the soil surface condition using the *Data Entry* worksheet (see appendix C-3). On the data form, record a "1" if the indicator is present and a "0" if the indicator or statement is absent, ending with a general Soil Disturbance Class (using table 3). For assistance with visual class determinations, use the *Soil Disturbance Field Guide* (Napper et al. N.d.). Continue collecting data at each monitoring point along the transect (grid). When you reach the edge of the activity area, select another transect direction (a predetermined grid point sampling scheme should be placed entirely within the activity area boundary) at an appropriate angle (toward the inside of the activity area) from the previous transect and continue data collection on the same spreadsheet. Note that, as you make observations at each monitoring point, the required sample size will likely change as the estimated variability changes.

Step 6. Continue the assessment until you reach the appropriate sample size. On the data form, record a "1" if the indicator is present and a "0" if the indicator or statement is absent, ending with a general soil disturbance class (table 2). *Take AT LEAST 30 monitoring points in the activity area that has disturbance.* Use aerial photos, ONSITE, or activity area maps to measure temporary roads and landings within or contiguous to the activity area, but take additional notes. Estimate disturbance on temporary roads or landings not in the activity area separately and manually add after completing this method.

Step 7. Use the comment field at the bottom of each column (or a field notebook) to document noteworthy existing disturbance. Use these comments to document unusual spatial features related to the disturbances or to record the type and severity of erosion features.

Step 8. In the last row of the *Data Entry* worksheet (see appendix C-3) indicate if the soil disturbance is detrimental. This row of information is based on the professional judgment of a qualified soil scientist, literature, or other local studies.

Postactivity Assessment

Step 1. Before starting work in an activity area, examine the soil in a nearby undisturbed unit for forest floor thickness, composition, mineral soil horizon depth(s), and depth to bedrock (if applicable). If baseline data have been collected (as in baseline assessment step 2), then this examination procedure may not be necessary. Examining an undisturbed area is essential, however, if one observer recorded the preactivity data and another observer is collecting the postactivity data. If an undisturbed site is not available, examine the undisturbed soil around stumps to become familiar with uncompacted soil conditions. Decide on the type of monitoring transect needed and locate a starting point using a method similar to that used for the preactivity assessment. It is not necessary to replicate transect locations from the previous assessment. The required sample size is likely to be different because of the increased variability of the site postactivity. It is better to complete two different assessments within the activity area.

Step 2. Using the procedure described for preactivity assessments, determine the soil surface disturbance. Record data points until you have taken enough monitoring points to reach the sample size calculated by the electronic spreadsheet or shown on the paper sample size table.

As in steps 7 and 8 (in the preactivity assessment), indicate the disturbance class for each point and indicate which points are considered detrimentally disturbed and would affect long-term site sustainability.

Interpreting the Results

Examples of questions that can be answered based on preactivity and postactivity soil disturbance assessments include the following:

1. How does soil disturbance differ from preactivity to postactivity?

2. What on-the-ground effects have resulted from the activity?

3. How do project effects compare to the effects predicted in the planning document?

4. Were soil mitigation measures implemented as planned and were they successful?

5. How does postactivity disturbance compare to the desired condition disclosed in the forest plan?

6. What mitigation measures would move soil resource conditions toward forest plan standards?

7. How and why did the soil disturbance classes change?

Definitions of Attributes and Indicators

Site Attributes

The following site attributes are entered into the electronic worksheet labeled *SoLo Info* (see appendix C-1). These site attributes are inserted into the worksheet during the "in the office" phase. Site attributes are described in detail in appendix G.

Soil Texture

Soil texture is a key property and allows for preassessment site stratification and later stratification of data results. Soil texture information is obtained from field examination. Although published soil surveys can be valuable resources, this information is often collected over too broad of a landscape and includes too many inclusions for site-specific assessment. Soil survey information needs to be verified in the activity area. Use standard techniques for identifying soil texture classes. The NRCS *Field Book for Describing and Sampling Soils* provides soil texture class definitions and techniques for classification (Schoeneberger et al. 1998). Soil texture information is recorded as sand, sandy loam, silt, loam, clay, and so on (as per the textural triangle). Soil texture often changes with depth and it is important to note these changes, particularly when describing soil displacement and erosion.

Soil moisture is critical when interpreting soil resistance to penetration as an affect of soil compaction. Record the soil moisture as dry, moist, or wet in the comment field of the *SoLo Info* worksheet. Dry soils have little to no moisture when examined in the field; in contrast, wet soils are saturated or nearly saturated and you can squeeze water out of them. Soil strength generally increases as the soil dries, so care must be taken when evaluating a soil for compaction if the soils are very dry. For example, a clayey soil can be very hard when dry, even if it is not compacted. Also, in some soils, massive structure may be more related to soil moisture than soil compaction from equipment operations. Note that compacted soils often stay moister longer than uncompacted soils, so, if clay is present, there could be a difference in penetration resistance related to the clay, not just compaction.

Information on coarse fragment percentage, size, and distribution within the surface soil is important when prescribing mitigation and restoration techniques. This information can be obtained from the local soil survey and verified in the field. Coarse fragments also determine the sensitivity of the soil to disturbance or its resiliency. The coarse fragment percentage class is categorized as <15% coarse fragments (no modifier, use the dominant texture), 15 to <35% (gravelly), 35 to <60% (very gravelly), 60 to <90% (extremely gravelly), >90% (no modifier, use the dominant size class; e.g., gravel). The size of coarse fragments is described as gravel (2 to <75 mm), cobble (75 to <250 mm), stone (250 to <600 mm), or boulders (>600 mm). The location of the coarse fragments is described as being mixed throughout the surface soils, limited to the A horizon, or limited to the B horizon or deeper (as estimated during a shovel test).

Textural class information does not need to be collected at every sample point but does need to be collected frequently enough to describe the heterogeneity or homogeneity of the activity area. The information on surface and subsurface texture is collected as a note and recorded on the *SoLo Info* worksheet (see appendix C-1).

Vegetation

Describing the vegetation provides insight about effective ground cover, changes in site productivity, and how well plants are using the soil resource. In the *SoLo Info* worksheet you can record the overall vegetation type (habitat type) and note any invasive or special species on the site. Information about the presence or absence of vegetative cover can be recorded at each sample point if desired. In addition, if a soil pit or other soil survey methods are used, information about root depth, location, abundance, and density can be recorded (Schoeneberger et al. 1998). These values can be collected for the activity area, along the transect (or grid points) at predetermined sample points (e.g., every 10 points) or when vegetation characteristics change.

Soil Structure

Soil structure is the naturally occurring arrangement of soil particles into aggregates. Most soil descriptions will include a note about structure (massive, granular, blocky, crumb, etc.) (Schoeneberger et al. 1998). Mechanical site treatments or prescribed fire may reduce these aggregates into smaller particles by the removal of organic matter or physical crushing. Mechanical treatments may also cause the structure to become massive (no structural units; material is a coherent mass) or puddled (soil smeared by machine traffic during wet conditions). The smaller particles created by physical crushing may alter infiltration, water and gas exchange, and biological processes. Although this site characteristic is often associated with the soil textural class, it can also be altered by harvest or site preparation activities. Overall, soil structure as related to the activity area and changes due to management should be noted on the *SoLo Info* worksheet (see appendix C-1).

Activity Area History

The attribute values for active area history are inserted into the *SoLo Info* worksheet and are collected once for each activity area when data are available. If these data are unavailable, insert a period (.) into the field. Providing activity area history also provides context for soil data interpretation. The values are collected once for every activity area. This information can be filled in during an office exercise before the field visit.

Soil Indicators

Soil indicators in the FSDMP were selected because they are fairly robust, could be used on a variety of sites, and are easy to define and recognize. Indicators can be turned "on" or "off" in the *Variable Selection* worksheet (see appendix C-2). All information about the following indicators is recorded as either a "1" (present) or a "0" (absent) on the *Data Entry* worksheet (see appendix C-3) within the 15-cm (6-in) sample point area. Figure 1 illustrates a harvest area with minimal soil surface effects.

Figure 1.—*Harvested stand with areas of class 0 disturbance.*

Machine Traffic Disturbances

Compaction and Bulk Density. The *Data Entry* worksheet (see appendix C-3) has three rows in which compaction are listed (by depth). Determine the maximum extent of compaction and record a "1" (present) in the appropriate cell for that sample point. The other two rows each will receive a "0" (absent). Indicators of change in compaction level are past operations (from aerial photos or databases), wheel tracks or depressions (ruts), equipment trails from more than two passes, excavated or bladed trails, penetration resistance, and a change in structure.

A metal rod or shovel can be inserted into the ground to determine changes in the compaction level of a sample point. This surrogate for bulk density sampling can be effective if undisturbed soils are nearby to calibrate this "push" test. All observers must calibrate themselves to the physical resistance of each soil type. Although a change in compaction is often measured by pushing a rod or spade into the soil (or taking a bulk density core), the visual attributes listed previously (wheel tracks, equipment trails, etc.) may be all that is necessary to determine a change in surface disturbance.

Placing compaction into a soil disturbance class—a 1, 2, or 3 (table 3)—is based on depth of compaction change into the mineral soil. Because of this depth relationship to the soil disturbance classes, it is important to know the undisturbed condition (at depths) of the soil preactivity.

Rutting and/or Wheel Track Impressions. The *Data Entry* worksheet (see appendix C-3 in volume II) has three rows in which ruts are listed (by depth). Determine the maximum extent of the rut and record a "1" (present) in the cell for that monitoring point. Record a "0" in each of the other two rows. To measure the depth of the rut, you may need to determine where the approximate surface of the undisturbed soil is (or was). As mentioned previously, you can measure these physical features for area (length multiplied by the average width) and enter them into ONSITE to determine areal extent.

Wheel tracks or ruts (impressions in the soil caused by heavy equipment) vary in depth and width. On sites that have a high compaction hazard (e.g., fine-textured soils, steep slopes), a shallow rut may cause degradation in site quality by altering the flow of water and gasses in the soil and/or increasing soil penetration resistance. On sites that have a low compaction hazard (e.g., coarse-textured soils), deeper ruts may not cause a detrimental change to water and gas flow but may represent displacement of fertile topsoil layers. Regardless of texture, however, wheel tracks and ruts can cause water to be routed off a site, making it unavailable for plant growth. Within a rut or wheel track could also be altered soil structure, increased soil density, puddling, compacted deposits of forest floor, fine slash, and woody debris (not readily excavated with a shovel). Placing ruts and wheel tracks into a soil disturbance category (disturbance class 1, 2, or 3) is based on their depth on the soil surface and their extension into the mineral soil profile. Figure 2 shows an example of a rut.

Figure 2.—*Example of a rut. Depth of rut will determine in which visual class this monitoring point would be placed.*

Soil Structure. Massive, platy, or puddled soil is recorded on the *Data Entry* worksheet in three separate rows. Determination of a change in structure is by depth and can sometimes be linked to the change in compaction level at the same depth. Determine the maximum extent of the change in structure and record a "1" (present) in the cell for that monitoring point. The other two cells for that monitoring point each will receive a "0" (absent).

Massive, platy, and puddled soil structure are indicators of a change in soil structure and a reduction in pore sizes that will change pore size distribution. Massive soil can be naturally occurring or can be caused by management activities. Massive structure means structural units are not present and the soil is a coherent mass. Platy structure can also be naturally occurring, but coarse-platy structure that has flat, or tabular-like ("dinner plate"), units within the profile is usually caused by harvesting equipment. Naturally occurring platy structure is not recorded in the field form; only management-induced changes in soil structure are recorded. Puddled soils are caused by equipment operating when the soil is too wet. Soil is smeared along a wheel track or rut and causes water to pond on the surface. The change in soil physical conditions and their depth into the mineral soil profile will determine into which soil disturbance class it is placed.

Surface Organic Matter. A row on the *Data Entry* worksheet (see appendix C-3) is for recording the depth of the forest floor (all surface organic horizons combined). Forest floor depth can be used to determine loss of nutrients from the organic layers. If the organic layers are piled and burned, nutrients are lost from the site. Page-Dumroese et al. (2000) describe how to use the NRCS soil data to determine approximate nutrient amounts and potential losses from organic matter changes due to site activity. Depending on site variability, this value can be collected for some (e.g., every 10 points) or all of the monitoring points. Measure the forest floor depth with a pocket ruler.

Displacement

Forest Floor. Displacement of the forest floor (all organic horizons above the mineral soil) is recorded on the *Data Entry* worksheet (see appendix C-3). The item on the worksheet reads "forest floor impacted." Record either a "0" (forest floor is not impacted) or a "1" (forest floor is impacted) in this row for each monitoring point. Large areas of displaced forest floor can lead to changes in nutrient cycling or erosion. Changes in the distribution and depth of the forest floor will change the soil disturbance severity rating. If the area of forest floor displacement is large, the area (length times average width) can be measured and entered into the ONSITE portion of the database to determine areal extent.

Mineral Soil. Record removal of the mineral soil is recorded under "Topsoil Displacement" in the *Data Entry* worksheet (see appendix C-3). Record either a "0" (displacement is absent) or a "1" (displacement is present) in this row for each monitoring point. Mineral soil displacement and gouging can result in degradation of site quality by exposing unfavorable subsoil material (e.g., denser, lower in nutrients, less organic matter, calcareous), altering slope hydrology and causing excessive erosion and, therefore, a loss of nutrients. Displacement that has removed most of the top mineral soil and exposed the subsoil is considered soil disturbance class 3 (fig. 3). See figure 4 for a schematic of several impacts in one location (rutting, displacement, and forest floor impacted). The effects of mineral

Figure 3.—*Example of combined rutting (foreground) and surface soil displacement (background).*

Figure 4.—*Schematic of surface soil displacement, rut, and forest floor impacted (from Napper et al. N.d.).*

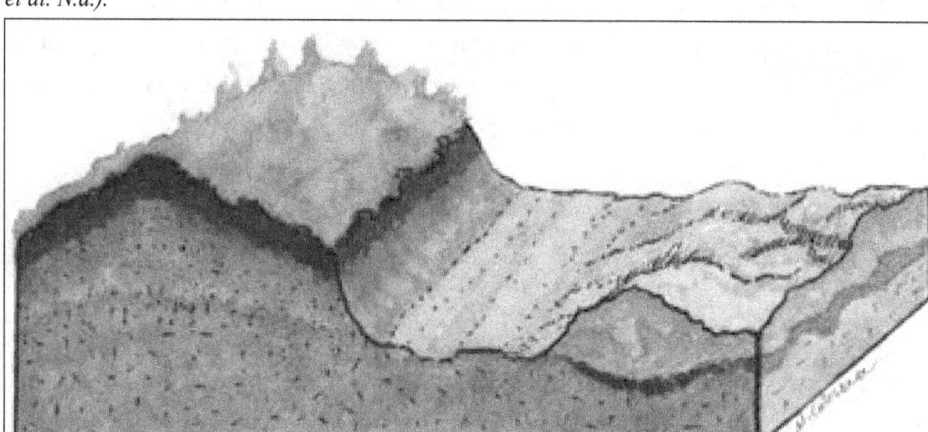

soil displacement on long-term productivity are governed by slope gradient, slope complexity, and subsoil conditions.

Changes in the soil disturbance categories are based on mixing of topsoil with the subsoil, topsoil removal, or evidence of gouging and piling. This attribute is the only one tied to an areal extent in some Forest Service regional soil quality standards and guidelines. Documentation should be made of the areal extent used by individuals before monitoring and should also be listed in the comment field. Because the electronic field form is used to calculate ongoing sample size using "0s" and "1s," areal extent size must be listed elsewhere. For example, if the displaced area is >1.5 m (5 ft) in diameter, then it is counted as "1" (present). Any area smaller than the selected areal extent is counted as "0" (absent). In addition, if areas of mineral topsoil displacement are extraordinarily large, they can be measured for area (length times average width) and entered into the ONSITE calculator.

Point Attributes

After recording information about forest floor impacted, use the section on the *Data Entry* worksheet (see appendix C-3) that asks for information about live plants, invasive species, fine woody material, coarse woody material, bare soil, and rock. These attributes are meant to help describe site conditions that may indicate a change in site sustainability or erosion potential. These attributes are not automatically included in the sample size calculation on the *Variable Selection* worksheet (see appendix C-2). If these attributes are important for particular sites, however, they may be included in the sample size calculation.

Erosion

Record erosion on the *Data Entry* worksheet (see appendix C-3) under "erosion." Record either a "0" (absent) or a "1" (present) in this row for each sample point. Soil erosion is the movement of soil by water and wind. Accelerated erosion (erosion caused by human activities that is more than the historic erosion rate) causes both onsite (soil loss, nutrient loss, lower productivity, and shallower mineral soil) and offsite (reduced stream water quality, increased sedimentation, and loss of habitat) effects.

Erosion noted in the FSDMP is for surface soils within an activity area. It is not designed for roads, ditches, or places where the subsoil is exposed. The degree and extent (slight, moderate, or severe) of erosion will place this attribute into different soil disturbance classes.

Prescribed Fire and Pile Burning

Prescribed fire severity is recorded on the *Data Entry* worksheet (see appendix C-3). The worksheet has three rows in which fire severity is listed (light, moderate, and severe). These levels of severity have been defined by the *Burned-Area Emergency Rehabilitation Handbook* (USDA Forest Service 1976). Determine the fire severity of the monitoring point and record a "1" (present) in the cell for that monitoring point. Record a "0" in the other two cells for that monitoring point.

Broadcast Burning. Broadcast burns across the activity area will probably create a mosaic of site conditions. Low-severity burns will probably not alter soil processes for an extensive period of time. Hotter burns may affect both the forest floor and mineral soil material. As burn intensity increases, the soil disturbance class (1, 2, or 3) also increases. As noted previously, the burn severity levels have already been defined. If burning is light (depth of char in the mineral soil <1 cm), then assign soil disturbance class 1. If burning is moderate (depth of char increases up to 5 cm), then assign disturbance class 2. Finally, if burning is severe (depth of char >5 cm), then assign disturbance class 3.

Pile Burning. Piles of waste logging materials, understory brush, small trees, or tree tops (slash) that remain after harvest activities are often burned within the activity area or on landings and skid trails. It may be difficult to describe conditions under the burned area if substantial slash remains, but it is critical to assess the size (width times length or diameter) of the area. ONSITE can be used to help calculate the size of these features. Because sample points land on different piles, assess them independently for severity. Assess the soil under the burn piles similarly to broadcast burning severity.

Assigning a Disturbance Class

Soil disturbance classes are identified using visual surface characteristics and are recorded for each point in the survey. The disturbances classes are defined in the above sections and table 2. Table 3 provides a listing of the soil visual indicators and how they may be associated with management activities. Data collected at each monitoring point provide a representative sample of the activity area. The percentage of the activity area in each soil disturbance class is calculated within the electronic spreadsheet (see the *Results* worksheet, appendix C-4). Reliability is estimated from the variance among estimated point proportions of each condition class. Some monitoring points may have a variety of soil disturbances. These overlapping indicators will have to be evaluated by the observer so that the soil disturbance class best represents the point sample (see figure 4).

Quality Assurance and Quality Control

A picture guide of the visual disturbance classes (Napper et al. N.d.) outlined in table 2 and a standardized training curriculum will be available by the end of 2009. Both of these efforts, plus the standardization of protocols and definitions, will help ensure that high-quality data are being collected consistently. In addition, regional soil program managers and forest soil scientists should conduct periodic local training for new employees using the FSDMP. Work is continuing on the national electronic database.

Glossary

activity area. A harvest unit, excluding system roads, as well as landings and temporary roads, outside the harvest unit boundary. An activity area may also be a prescribed burn unit or any area delineated on the ground for a specific treatment.

areal extent. The measured area (length times width or diameter) affected by any activity.

biological indicators of soil quality. Measures of living organisms or their activity used as indicators of soil quality. Measuring soil organisms can be done in three general ways:

1. Counting soil organisms or measuring microbial biomass.

2. Measuring biologic activity (e.g., soil basal respiration, cotton strip assay, or potentially mineralizable nitrogen).

3. measuring diversity, such as diversity of functions (e.g., BIOLOG plates) or diversity of chemical structure (e.g., cell components, fatty acids, or DNA).

chemical indicators of soil quality. Indicators that include tests of organic matter, pH, electrical conductivity, heavy metals, cation exchange capacity, and other parameters.

dynamic soil quality. An aspect of soil quality relating to soil properties that change as a result of soil use and management or over the human time scale.

erosion. The detachment and movement of soil or rock by water, wind, ice, or gravity.

forest floor. All organic soil horizons consisting of dead plant material on the surface of the mineral soil surface.

inherent soil quality. An aspect of soil quality relating to a soil's natural composition and properties as influenced by the factors and processes of soil formation in the absence of human effects.

physical indicators of soil disturbance. Characteristics that vary with management and that include bulk density, aggregate stability, infiltration, hydraulic conductivity, and penetration resistance.

platy soil structure. The arrangement of soil particles into aggregates that is flat horizontally. Platy structure can be natural or caused by trafficking.

puddling. The destruction of soil structure and the associated loss of macro porosity that results from working on a soil that is wet.

soil function. Any service, role, or task that soil performs, especially the following:

1. Sustaining biological activity, diversity, and productivity.

2. Regulating and partitioning water and solute flow (hydrologic function).

3. Filtering, buffering, degrading, and detoxifying potential pollutants.

4. Storing and cycling nutrients.

5. Providing support for buildings and other structures (trees) and protecting archaeological treasures (cultural features).

soil quality. The capacity of a specific kind of soil to function, within natural or managed ecosystem boundaries, to sustain plant and animal productivity, maintain or enhance water and air quality, and support human health and habitation and ecosystem health. Two aspects of the definition are dynamic soil quality and inherent soil quality.

soil quality indicator. A quantitative or qualitative measure used to estimate soil functional capacity. Indicators should be adequately sensitive to change, accurately reflect the processes or biophysical mechanisms relevant to the function of interest, and be cost effective and relatively easy and practical to measure. Soil quality indicators are often categorized into biological, chemical, and physical indicators.

soil quality monitoring. The act of tracking trends in quantitative indicators or the functional capacity of the soil to determine the success of, or changes associated with, management practices (land uses or disturbances) or the need for additional management changes. Monitoring involves the orderly collection, analysis, and interpretation of data from the same locations over time.

Literature Cited

Block, R.; Van Rees, K.C.J.; Pennock, D.J. 2002. Quantifying harvesting impacts using soil compaction and disturbance regimes at a landscape scale. Soil Science Society of America Journal. 66: 1669–1676.

Burger, J.A.; Kelting, D.L. 1998. Soil quality monitoring for assessing sustainable forest management. In: Adams, M.B.; Ramakrishna, K.; Davidson, E., eds. The contribution of soil science to the development and implementation of criteria and indicators of sustainable forest management. SSSA Spec. Publ. 53. Madison, WI: Soil Science Society of America: 17–53.

Burger, J.A.; Kelting, D.L. 1999. Using soil quality indicators to assess forest stand management. Forest Ecology and Management. 122: 155–166.

Busse, M.D.; Beattie, S.E.; Powers, R.F., et al. 2006. Microbial community responses in forest mineral soil to compaction, organic matter removal, and vegetation control. Canadian Journal of Forest Research. 36: 577–588.

Clayton, J.L.; Kellogg, G.; Forrester, N. 1987. Soil disturbance-tree growth relations in central Idaho clearcuts. Research Note INT-372. Ogden, UT: U.S. Department of Agriculture, Forest Service, Intermountain Research Station. 6 p.

Cochran, P.H.; Brock, T. 1985. Soil compaction and initial height growth of planted ponderosa pine. Research Note PNW-434. Portland, OR: U.S. Department of Agriculture, Forest Service, Pacific Northwest Forest and Range Experiment Station. 10 p.

Craigg, T.L.; Howes, S.W. 2007. Assessing quality in volcanic ash soils. In: Page-Dumroese, D.S.; Miller, R.E.; Mital, J., et al., tech. eds. Volcanic-ash-derived forest soils of the Inland Northwest: properties and implications for management and restoration. Proceedings, Volcanic-Ash-Derived Forest Soils of the Inland Northwest: Properties and Implications for Management and Restoration. RMRS-P-44. Fort Collins, CO: U.S. Department of Agriculture, Forest Service, Rocky Mountain Research Station: 47–67.

Curran, M.; Maynard, D.; Heninger, R., et al. 2007. Elements and rationale for a common approach to assess and report soil disturbance. The Forestry Chronicle. 83: 852–866.

Curran, M.P., Miller, R.E.; Howes, S.W., et al. 2005. Progress toward more uniform assessment and reporting of soil disturbance for operations, research, and sustainability protocols. Forest Ecology and Management. 220: 7–30.

Doran, J.W.; Parkin, T.B. 1994. Defining and assessing soil quality. In: Doran, J.W.; Coleman, D.C.; Bezdicek, D.F., et al., eds. Defining soil quality for a sustainable environment. SSSA Spec. Pub. 35. Madison, WI: Soil Science Society of America: 3–11.

Fleming, R.L.; Powers, R.F.; Foster, N.W., et al. 2006. Effects of organic matter removal, soil compaction, and vegetation control on 5-year seedling performance: a regional comparison of Long-Term Soil Productivity sites. Canadian Journal of Forest Research. 36: 5429–5450.

Froehlich, H.A. 1976. The influence of different thinning systems on damage to soil and trees. Proceedings, XVI IUFRO World Congress Division IV. Oslo, Norway: International Union of Forest Research Organizations: 333–334.

Gomez, A.; Powers, R.F.; Singer, M.J., et al. 2002. Soil compaction effects on growth of young ponderosa pine following litter removal in California's Sierra Nevada. Soil Science Society of America Journal. 66: 1334–1343.

Heninger, R.; Scott, W.; Dobkowski, A., et al. 2002. Soil disturbance and 10-year growth response of coast Douglas-fir on nontilled and tilled skid trails in the Oregon Cascades. Canadian Journal of Forest Research. 32: 233–246.

Herrick, J.E.; VanZee, J.W.; Havstad, K.M., et al. 2005. Monitoring manual for grassland, shrubland and savanna ecosystems. Vol. I: Quick start. Las Cruces, NM: U.S. Department of Agriculture, Agricultural Research Service Jornada Experimental Range. 36 p.

Howes, S.; Hazard, J.; Geist, J.M. 1983. Guidelines for sampling some physical conditions of surface soils. R6-RWM-146-1983. Portland, OR: U.S. Department of Agriculture, Forest Service, Pacific Northwest Region. 34 p.

Howes, S.W. 2006. Soil disturbance monitoring in the USDA Forest Service, Pacific Northwest Region. Proceedings, Monitoring Science and Technology Symposium: Unifying Knowledge for Sustainability in the Western Hemisphere. RMRS-P-42CD. Fort Collins, CO: U.S. Department of Agriculture, Forest Service, Rocky Mountain Research Station: 929–935.

Laing, L.E.; Howes, S.W. 1988. Detrimental soil compaction resulting from a feller buncher and rubber-tired skidder timber harvest operation: a case study. In: Lousier, J.D.; Still, G.W., eds. Degradation of forested lands: forest soils at risk. Proceedings, 10th B.C. Soil Science Workshop. 191–195.

Larson, W.E.; Pierce, F.J. 1994. The dynamics of soil quality as a measure of sustainable management. In: Doran, J.W.; Coleman, D.C.; Bezdicek, D.F., et al., eds. Defining soil quality for a sustainable environment. SSSA Spec. Pub. 35. Madison, WI: Soil Science Society of America: 37–51.

McNab, W.H.; Cleland, D.T.; Freeouf, J.A., et al., comps. 2007. Description of ecological subregions: sections of the conterminous United States [CD-ROM]. Gen. Tech. Rep. WO-76B. Washington, DC: U.S. Department of Agriculture, Forest Service. 80 p.

Morris, L.A.; Miller, R.E. 1994. Evidence for long-term productivity change as provided by field trials. In: Dyck, W.J., ed. Impacts of forest harvesting on long-term site productivity. London, United Kingdom: Chapman & Hall 41–80.

Napper, C.; Howes, S.; Page-Dumroese, D. [N.d.]. Soil disturbance field guide. Manuscript in preparation. 0820 1815-SDTDC. San Dimas, CA: San Dimas Technology Center.

Page-Dumroese, D.; Jurgensen, M.; Abbott, A., et al. 2006. Monitoring changes in soil quality from postfire logging in the Inland Northwest. In: Andrews, P.L.; Butler, B.W., comps. Proceedings, Fuels Management: How To Measure Success. RM-P-41. Ft. Collins, CO: U.S. Department of Agriculture, Forest Service, Rocky Mountain Research Station: 605–614.

Page-Dumroese, D.; Jurgensen, M.; Elliot, W., et al. 2000. Soil quality standards and guidelines for forest sustainability in northwestern North America. Forest Ecology and Management. 138: 445–462.

Page-Dumroese, D.S.; Jurgensen, M.F.; Tiarks, A.E., et al. 2006. Soil physical property changes at North American Long-Term Soil Productivity study sites: 1 and 5 years after compaction. Canadian Journal of Forest Research. 36: 551–564.

Powers, R.F.; Alban, D.H.; Miller, R.E., et al. 1990. Sustaining site productivity in North American forests: problems and prospects. In: Gessel, S.P.; Lacate, D.S.; Weetman, G.F., et al., eds. Sustained productivity of forest soils. Proceedings, 7th North American Forest Soils Conference. Vancouver, British Columbia: University British Columbia, Faculty of Forestry: 49–79.

Powers, R.F.; Scott, D.A.; Sanchez, F.G., et al. 2005. The North American long-term soil productivity experiment: findings from the first decade of research. Forest Ecology and Management. 220: 17–30.

Powers, R.F.; Tiarks, A.E.; Boyle, J.R. 1998. Assessing soil quality: practical standards for sustainable forest productivity in the United States. In: Adams, M.B.; Ramakrishna, K.; Davidson, E., eds. The contribution of soil science to the development and implementation of criteria and indicators of sustainable forest management. SSSA Spec. Publ. 53. Madison, WI: Soil Science Society of America: 53–80.

Sanchez, F.G.; Scott, D.A.; Ludovici, K.H. 2006. Negligible effects of severe organic matter removal and soil compaction on loblolly pine growth over 10 years. Forest Ecology and Management. 227: 145–154.

Schoeneberger, P.J.; Wysocki, D.A.; Benham, E.C., et al. 1998. Field book for describing and sampling soils. Lincoln, NE: U.S. Department of Agriculture, Natural Resources Conservation Service, National Soil Survey Center.

Sheaffer, R.L.; Mendenhall, W.; Ott, L. 1996. Elementary survey sampling. 5th ed. Belmont, CA: Wadsworth Publishing. 72 p.

Snider, M.D.; Miller, R.F. 1985. Effects of tractor logging on soils and vegetation in eastern Oregon. Soil Science Society of America Journal. 49: 1280–1282.

Staddon, J.W.; Duchesne, L.C.; Trevors, J.T. 1999. The role of microbial indicators of soil quality in ecological forest management. The Forestry Chronicle. 75: 81–86.

Sullivan, T.E. 1987. Monitoring soil physical conditions on a national forest in Eastern Oregon. In: Slaughter, G.W.; Gasbarro, T., eds. Proceedings, Alaskan Forest Soil Productivity Workshop. Gen. Tech. Rep. PNW-GTR-219. Portland, OR: U.S. Department of Agriculture, Forest Service, Pacific Northwest Forest and Range Experiment Station: 69–76.

Triola, M.F. 2001. Elementary statistics. 8th ed. Upper Saddle River, NJ: Addison Wesley Longman, Inc. 855 p.

U.S. Department of Agriculture (USDA) Forest Service. 1976. Burned-area emergency rehabilitation handbook. FSH 2509.13. Washington, DC: U.S. Department of Agriculture, Forest Service. 115 p.

USDA Forest Service. 1983. The principal laws relating to Forest Service activities. Agricultural handbook 453. Washington, DC: U.S. Department of Agriculture, Forest Service. 591 p.

U.S. Department of Agriculture (USDA) Natural Resources Conservation Service (NRCS). 1993. Soil survey manual. Rev. Agricultural handbook 18. Washington, DC: U.S. Department of Agriculture, Natural Resources Conservation Service, Soil Survey Staff. 437 p.

Warkentin, B.P. 1995. The changing concept of soil quality. Journal of Soil and Water Conservation. 50: 226–228.

Appendix A. Options for Monitoring Point Layout

For each option listed below, a minimum of 30 monitoring points is required to calculate the remainder of the sample size.

Option 1. Randomly Oriented Transects

Established transects. Pre-established grid (randomly oriented) with transects oriented along random azimuths. Transects are of standard length, usually 100 ft.

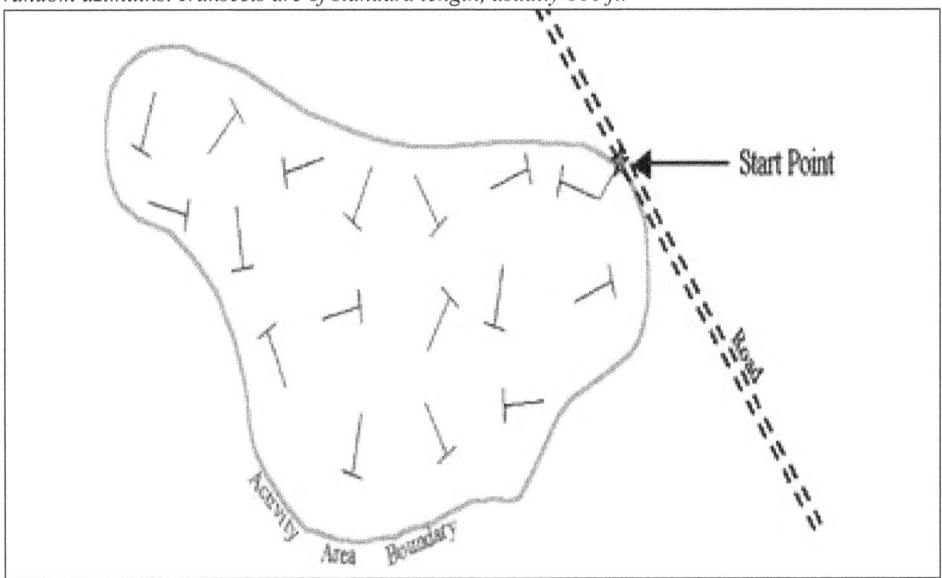

In this option, transects are laid out randomly on a site map before going to the field. Monitoring points can be collected along these randomly established transects to collect the minimum number of points needed. At each intersection, a 30-m (~100-ft) transect is established. The attributes are then noted at monitoring points located along each transect.

Option 2. Systematic Grid Points

In this option, the protocol calls for establishing a systematic grid of monitoring points arrayed on a map or aerial photograph of the activity area to be monitored. The entire grid is randomly located and oriented, and the distance between monitoring points is constructed to provide a sample size that meets precision requirements or cost limitations specified in the objectives for monitoring. Each grid intersection locates a monitoring point that radiates in a random chosen direction and distance from the grid point (Howes 2006).

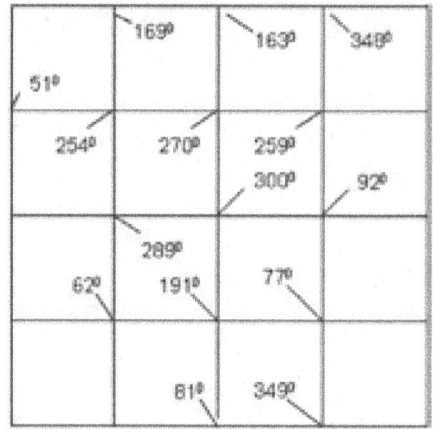

Option 3. A Random Transect

In this option, the protocol calls for randomly locating a start point and traversing a transect that covers the entire unit so that the first 30 monitoring points (the minimum required) are spaced to provide an adequate assessment of the site. The entire transect is randomly located and oriented, and the distance between monitoring points is constructed to provide a sample size that meets precision requirements or cost limitations specified in the objectives for monitoring. Turning points are usually located within the activity area so that the last monitoring point before a turn is not within an area of influence of the surrounding stand (usually the height of the tallest trees). Additional transects at random directions are often needed to reach the appropriate sample size. If the transect begins to follow a skid road, either offset from the skid road or start a new random transect. Record offset or new direction.

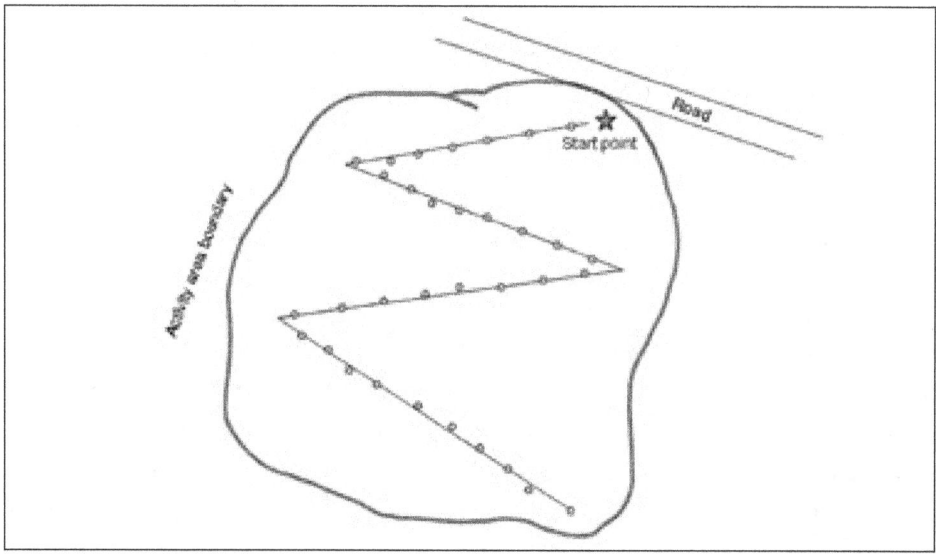

Appendix B. Statistical Background of the Forest Soil Disturbance Monitoring Protocol

The goal of the data collection process using the Forest Soil Disturbance Monitoring Protocol (FSDMP) is to obtain a representative estimate of the amount and types of management-induced disturbance within a particular activity area. Although there is a "true" proportion of any area that is disturbed, the only way to determine that true proportion would be to measure every possible point within the entire activity area. Because monitoring every point is impossible, given time and budget constraints, a sample of monitoring points must be taken. When the sample is chosen randomly (every possible monitoring point within the area has the same probability of being chosen) and "large enough," it can be considered representative of the activity area as a whole.

A large enough sample is determined by first specifying the confidence level that is acceptable for the monitoring estimate. As the level of confidence increases, so does the number of monitoring points necessary to estimate the disturbance (assuming that the variability stays constant). The confidence level can be chosen by the user in consultation with a line officer if necessary. The confidence level is specified within either the *SoLo Info* or *Data Entry* worksheets (see appendixes C-1 and C-3, respectively) or by choosing the appropriate column on the sample size tables (see appendixes D-2 and D-3), and then finding the associated sample size for a given proportion of disturbed monitoring points. At this time, available confidence levels within the electronic worksheets range from 70 to 95 percent. The margin of error around each estimate is either ± 5 or ±10 percent (with an overall confidence width of ±10 or ±20), meaning that, after the proportion of disturbance for a particular variable is estimated for the activity area, the interval calculated by taking the sample proportion ±5 percent (or ±10 percent) will contain the true proportion with the chosen level of confidence. The sample size tables also contain information to calculate sample size with confidence levels from 70 to 95 percent. Sample size information with the margin of error at ±5 percent is found in appendix D-2. Sample size information with the margin of error at ±10 percent sample size calculations is in appendix D-3.

The sample size required to estimate the proportion of disturbance is first calculated individually for each indicator variable. The overall sample size that should be used for monitoring is the largest of the individual sample sizes to ensure that the margin of error is within acceptable limits for every indicator variable. Sample sizes are not dependent on the size of the activity area; they are dependent *only* on the level of confidence and the amount of variability estimated from the sample points within an activity area. The procedure outlined here is a point sample and, within any size activity area, the number of potential points to sample is infinite.

All the indicator variables that contribute to the overall sample size calculation are *binomial* variables, meaning they can take on *only* one of two values: either the characteristic is "1" (present) or "0" (absent.) When the sample size is at least 30, the normal approximation to the binomial distribution can be used (Triola 2001]). Using binary variables as the basis for the sample size determination has several advantages (Sheaffer et al. 1996). The maximum possible variability for any site is a fixed number that is reached when 50 percent of the monitoring points have the characteristic and 50 percent do not. Using binary variables allows for variability to be estimated and sample size calculated in the field on a single sampling trip with a simple set of calculations. The FSDMP uses a minimum of 30 monitoring points from the initial transect as the "pilot" data for any given area and thus ensures that the sample size necessary for each area is based on accurate variability estimates within that area.

The required sample size for each indicator variable is calculated according to the following formula:

$$n = \frac{(z_{\alpha/2})^2 * \hat{p} * \hat{q}}{w^2}$$

Variables within this formula are as follows:

- $z_{\alpha/2}$ is the standard normal percentile yielding the chosen confidence level. The user must specify the desired confidence level within the electronic data entry spreadsheet or choose the appropriate column from the sample size tables (see appendixes D-2 and D-3).

- $\hat{p}$ is the observed proportion of monitoring points that have disturbance and are marked "present" by recording a "1." This proportion is computed by adding the total number of "1s" and dividing by the total number of monitoring points. The electronic spreadsheet will perform this calculation automatically; however, those using a paper copy of the electronic form (see appendix D-1) must calculate this proportion in the field.

- $\hat{q}$ is the observed proportion of monitoring points that do not have disturbance and are marked "absent" by recording a "0." This proportion is computed by adding the total number of "0s" and dividing by the total number of monitoring points or by subtracting $\hat{p}$ (as found above) from 1 since $\hat{p} + \hat{q} = 1$.

- w is the 1/2-width of the confidence interval. At this time, the sample sizes are calculated based on a confidence-interval width of 10 percent (or 20 percent), which will result in the estimates with a plus or minus 5 percent (or 10 percent) margin of error.

For example, with an 80-percent confidence level, at the calculated sample size, the confidence interval given by the range $\hat{p} \pm 5\%$ will have "captured" the true proportion of disturbed points in the activity area 80 percent of the time.

The *minimum* number of monitoring points is 30. This minimum number is required when using the above formula to calculate sample size and confidence intervals. If fewer than 30 monitoring points are taken, the sample sizes and confidence intervals calculated within the spreadsheet will be incorrect. The consequence of using more than 30 samples but fewer than the number recommended by the sample size calculator within the electronic spreadsheet or on a paper copy of the electronic form (see appendix D-1) is that the confidence interval may be wider, as indicated by the "Lower Bound" and "Upper Bound" values on the spreadsheet (see *Results* worksheet, appendix C-4).

The confidence intervals calculated on the electronic spreadsheet are the actual confidence intervals from the initial monitoring data along the sampling transect and may be used as summary data for reporting. For those using the paper copy of the electronic form (see appendix D-1), we suggest entering the data into the electronic spreadsheet to obtain the intervals with no manual calculation. The formulas for the lower and upper bounds of the confidence intervals are as follows:

$$\text{Lower Bound} = \hat{p} - z_{\alpha/2} \sqrt{\frac{\hat{p} * \hat{q}}{n}}$$

$$\text{Upper Bound} = \hat{p} + z_{\alpha/2} \sqrt{\frac{\hat{p} * \hat{q}}{n}}$$

where the variables are previously defined for the sample size formula. The values for $z_{\alpha/2}$ are shown here:

Confidence Level	$z_{\alpha/2}$
70%	1.04
75%	1.15
80%	1.282
85%	1.44
90%	1.645
95%	1.96

In the electronic spreadsheet on the tab labeled *Results* (see appendix C-4), the estimated proportion of disturbance for the area is shown along with the lower and upper bounds of the confidence interval for each indicator variable. These values are provided for convenience in final reporting. The correct interpretation of the confidence intervals can be illustrated with the following example: if an activity area yields a $\hat{p}$ for the indicator variable "rutting <5cm" of 0.1545 and the required sample size of 109 (from an

85-percent confidence level) was met by taking 110 monitoring points, the lower bound is 0.104916 and the upper bound is 0.204175. This example shows that, with 85-percent confidence, the interval (0.1, 0.2) has captured the true proportion of rutting less than 5 cm within this particular activity area. It should be noted that intervals calculated for low levels of disturbance (less than 5 percent) are truncated to have a lower bound of zero because negative values are impossible.

Summary levels of disturbance classes are also provided within the electronic *Data Entry* spreadsheet (see appendix C-3). Because this variable is ordinal (meaning that levels of this variable are ordered categories), confidence intervals may not be calculated.

Appendix C. Examples of Worksheets Contained in the Forest Soil Disturbance Monitoring Protocol Spreadsheet

Appendix C-1. Example Worksheet for Collecting Soil Disturbance Monitoring Data (SoLo Info)

The first tab of the electronic spreadsheet is a worksheet labeled *SoLo Info* (shown below). Use this worksheet to describe the site attributes. Additional details of the information requested in this worksheet are described in appendix G. In the Indicator section of this worksheet, #DIV/0! will be automatically filled in when the *Data Entry (*see appendix C-3) worksheet is completed.

SoLo Soil Quality Monitoring Report:	
Site Identification:	
Project ID:	
Unit ID:	
Subunit ID:	
Project Type:	
Other (Comment):	
Location Information	
Region:	
Forest:	
District:	
USGS Quad(s):	
Section(s):	
Township:	
Range:	
Meridian:	
Latitude:	0.000000
Longitude:	0.000000
Datum:	0
UTM Easting:	0
UTM Northing:	0
UTM Zone:	0
GIS Coverage:	
Polygon ID:	
Site Characteristics:	
Slope (%):	
Aspect (degrees or direction):	
Elevation (feet? meters?):	
Area (acres? hectares?):	
Ecological Subsection:	
Landform/Topography:	
Habitat Type:	
Watershed Name:	
Watershed HUC:	
Watershed Condition Class:	
Landtype Association:	
Parent Material:	
Soil Classification:	
Soil Survey:	
Comments:	

Site History:	
Wildfire (season & year):	
Grazing (span of years):	
Harvest (season & year):	
Harvest System:	
Site Prep (including Rx fire):	
Planted (year):	
Thinned (year):	
Recreational Use:	
Roading (miles/kilometers):	
Deroading:	
Other Reclamation:	
Other (Comment):	
Current Activity:	
Prescription (treatment):	
Method/System:	
Monitoring Type:	
Confidence Level Selected:	95
Confidence Interval Selected:	10
Number of Points in Survey:	0
Indicator:	**Proportion Positive**
Forest Floor Impacted:	#DIV/0!
Displacement:	#DIV/0!
Erosion:	#DIV/0!
Rutting:	#DIV/0!
Burning:	#DIV/0!
Compaction:	#DIV/0!
Platy/Massive/Puddled:	#DIV/0!
Other (Comment):	
Administrative Information:	
Observer:	
Observer Title:	
Observer E-mail:	
Date Monitored:	1/0/1900
Date Approved:	
Approver:	
Approver Title:	
Approver E-mail:	
Date Reported:	
NEPA Document:	
Date NEPA Completed:	

GIS = Geographic Information System. HUC = Hydrologic Unit
Code. NEPA = National Environmental Policy Act. UTM = Universal
Transverse Mercator.

Appendix C-2. Example Worksheet for Collecting Soil Disturbance Monitoring Results (Variable Selection)

The second tab of the electronic spreadsheet for data collection is the worksheet labeled *Variable Selection* and is shown below. Changing the entries for any particular variable from 1 to 0 results in those variables being excluded in the sample size calculation; however, summary statistics and confidence intervals will still be calculated.

Select the variables to be included in the sample size calculation
Enter 1 to include
Enter 0 to exclude

Forest Floor Impacted?	1
Live Plant?	0
Invasive Plant?	0
Fine Woody? <7 cm	0
Coarse Woody? >7cm	0
Bare Soil?	0
Rock?	0
Topsoil Displacement?	1
Erosion? Comment!	1
Rutting? <5cm	1
Rutting? 5-10cm	1
Rutting? >10cm	1
Burning Light	1
Burning Moderate	1
Burning Severe	1
Compaction? 0-10 cm	1
Compaction? > 10-30 cm	1
Compaction? >30 cm	1
Platy/Massive/Puddled Structure 0-10 cm	1
Platy/Massive/Puddled Structure >10-30 cm	1
Platy/Massive/Puddled Structure >30 cm	1

Appendix C-3. Example Worksheet for Collecting Soil Disturbance Monitoring Results (Data Entry)

The third tab of the electronic spreadsheet for data collection is a worksheet labeled *Data Entry*. Record either "0" (absent) or "1" (present) in each cell of the spreadsheet **except** for forest floor depth. Forest floor depth is recorded in centimeters.

NOTE: This spreadsheet example contains only 23 data points.

Project ID:										0			Unit ID:			0		Observer:			0				0	
Date:					Monitoring Type:								0											Point Spacing (m):		
Direction:																										
Sample point	1	2	3	4	5	6	7	8	9	10	11	12	13	14	15	16	17	18	19	20	21	22	23			
f. floor depth (cm):																										
Forest floor Impacted?																										
Live Plant?																										
Invasive Plant?																										
Fine Woody? <7 cm																										
Coarse Woody? >7cm																										
Bare Soil?																										
Rock?																										
Topsoil displacement?																										
Erosion?, comment!																										
Rutting? <5cm																										
Rutting? 5-10cm																										
Rutting? >10cm																										
Burning light																										
Burning moderate																										
Burning severe																										

Compaction? 0-10 cm	Compaction? 10-30 cm	Compaction? >30cm	Platy/Massive/Puddled structure 0-10 cm	Platy/Massive/Puddled structure 10-30 cm	Platy/Massive/Puddled structure >30 cm		N Needed (round UP)	#DIV/0!	Estimated Soil Disturbance Class	Detrimental? Enter 1 if Yes, 0 if No	Comments

Appendix C-4. Example Worksheet for Collecting Soil Disturbance Monitoring Results (Results)

The fourth tab of the electronic spreadsheet for data collection is a worksheet labeled *Results*. Note that as columns in the *Data Entry* tab are filled out, the "#DIV/0!" will be replaced with the calculated results.

Activity Area and Transect:				
Date:	1/0/1900			
	Visual		Confidence Intervals	
Sample point	Class		Lower	Upper
f. floor depth (cm):	Proportions	N needed	Bound	Bound
Forest floor Impacted?	#DIV/0!	#DIV/0!	#DIV/0!	#DIV/0!
Live Plant?	#DIV/0!	#DIV/0!	#DIV/0!	#DIV/0!
Invasive Plant?	#DIV/0!	#DIV/0!	#DIV/0!	#DIV/0!
Fine Woody? <7 cm	#DIV/0!	#DIV/0!	#DIV/0!	#DIV/0!
Coarse Woody? >7cm	#DIV/0!	#DIV/0!	#DIV/0!	#DIV/0!
Bare Soil?	#DIV/0!	#DIV/0!	#DIV/0!	#DIV/0!
Rock?	#DIV/0!	#DIV/0!	#DIV/0!	#DIV/0!
Topsoil displacement?	#DIV/0!	#DIV/0!	#DIV/0!	#DIV/0!
Erosion?, comment!	#DIV/0!	#DIV/0!	#DIV/0!	#DIV/0!
Rutting? <5cm	#DIV/0!	#DIV/0!	#DIV/0!	#DIV/0!
Rutting? 5-10cm	#DIV/0!	#DIV/0!	#DIV/0!	#DIV/0!
Rutting? >10cm	#DIV/0!	#DIV/0!	#DIV/0!	#DIV/0!
Burning light	#DIV/0!	#DIV/0!	#DIV/0!	#DIV/0!
Burning moderate	#DIV/0!	#DIV/0!	#DIV/0!	#DIV/0!
Burning severe	#DIV/0!	#DIV/0!	#DIV/0!	#DIV/0!
Compaction? 0-10 cm	#DIV/0!	#DIV/0!	#DIV/0!	#DIV/0!
Compaction? 10-30 cm	#DIV/0!	#DIV/0!	#DIV/0!	#DIV/0!
Compaction? >30cm	#DIV/0!	#DIV/0!	#DIV/0!	#DIV/0!
Platy/Massive/Puddled structure 0-10 cm	#DIV/0!	#DIV/0!	#DIV/0!	#DIV/0!
Platy/Massive/Puddled structure 10-30 cm	#DIV/0!	#DIV/0!	#DIV/0!	#DIV/0!
Platy/Massive/Puddled structure >30 cm	#DIV/0!	#DIV/0!	#DIV/0!	#DIV/0!
	Soil Disturbance Class Proportions			
Estimated Soil Disturbance Class	Proportion 0's	Proportion 1's	Proportion 2's	Proportion 3's	total
	#DIV/0!	#DIV/0!	#DIV/0!	#DIV/0!	0
Detrimental (Proportion Yes)	#DIV/0!			

Appendix D. Paper Field Form and Tables for Determining Sample Size

Appendix D-1. Example of Paper Field Form

Note: This form contains only 30 sample points.

Activity Area and Transect:											Forest/Unit:						Observer:										Confidence level? Enter 80, 90 or 95			
Date:									Treatment:										Point Spacing (m):											
Sample point	1	2	3	4	5	6	7	8	9	10	11	12	13	14	15	16	17	18	19	20	21	22	23	24	25	26	27	28	29	30
f. floor depth (cm):																														
Forest floor Impacted?																														
Topsoil displacement?																														
Mixed topsoil/subsoil?																														
Erosion?, comment!																														
Rutting? <5cm																														
Rutting? 5-10cm																														
Rutting? >10cm																														
Burning light																														
Burning moderate																														
Burning severe																														

Compaction? 0-10 cm	Compaction? 10-30 cm	Compaction? >30cm	Platy/Massive structure 0-10 cm	Platy/Massive structure 10-30 cm	Platy/Massive structure >30 cm	Live Plant?	Fine Woody? <7 cm	Coarse Woody? >7cm	Bare Soil?	Rock?	Estimated Soil Disturbance Class	Detrimental? Yes/No	Comments (Right Click and Use Insert Comment)

Appendix D-2. Determining Sample Size With a Margin of Error at ± 5 Percent

70% Confidence		75% Confidence		80% Confidence		85% Confidence		90% Confidence		95% Confidence	
Percent Present	N Required	Percent Present	N Required	Percent Present	N Required	Percent Present	N Required	Percent Present	N Required	Percent Present	N Required
1%	5	1%	6	1%	7	1%	9	1%	11	1%	16
2%	9	2%	11	2%	13	2%	17	2%	22	2%	31
3%	13	3%	16	3%	20	3%	25	3%	32	3%	45
4%	17	4%	21	4%	26	4%	32	4%	42	4%	60
5%	21	5%	26	5%	32	5%	40	5%	52	5%	73
6%	25	6%	30	6%	37	6%	47	6%	62	6%	87
7%	29	7%	35	7%	43	7%	54	7%	71	7%	101
8%	32	8%	39	8%	49	8%	62	8%	80	8%	114
9%	36	9%	44	9%	54	9%	68	9%	89	9%	126
10%	39	10%	48	10%	59	10%	75	10%	98	10%	139
11%	43	11%	52	11%	65	11%	82	11%	106	11%	151
12%	46	12%	56	12%	70	12%	88	12%	115	12%	163
13%	49	13%	60	13%	75	13%	94	13%	123	13%	174
14%	53	14%	64	14%	79	14%	100	14%	131	14%	186
15%	56	15%	68	15%	84	15%	106	15%	139	15%	196
16%	59	16%	72	16%	89	16%	112	16%	146	16%	207
17%	62	17%	75	17%	93	17%	118	17%	153	17%	217
18%	64	18%	79	18%	97	18%	123	18%	160	18%	227
19%	67	19%	82	19%	101	19%	128	19%	167	19%	237
20%	70	20%	85	20%	105	20%	133	20%	174	20%	246
21%	72	21%	88	21%	109	21%	138	21%	180	21%	255
22%	75	22%	91	22%	113	22%	143	22%	186	22%	264
23%	77	23%	94	23%	117	23%	147	23%	192	23%	273
24%	79	24%	97	24%	120	24%	152	24%	198	24%	281
25%	82	25%	100	25%	123	25%	156	25%	203	25%	289
26%	84	26%	102	26%	127	26%	160	26%	209	26%	296
27%	86	27%	105	27%	130	27%	164	27%	214	27%	303
28%	88	28%	107	28%	133	28%	168	28%	219	28%	310
29%	90	29%	109	29%	135	29%	171	29%	223	29%	317
30%	91	30%	112	30%	138	30%	175	30%	228	30%	323
31%	93	31%	114	31%	141	31%	178	31%	232	31%	329
32%	95	32%	116	32%	143	32%	181	32%	236	32%	335
33%	96	33%	117	33%	145	33%	184	33%	240	33%	340
34%	98	34%	119	34%	148	34%	187	34%	243	34%	345
35%	99	35%	121	35%	150	35%	189	35%	247	35%	350
36%	100	36%	122	36%	151	36%	192	36%	250	36%	355
37%	101	37%	124	37%	153	37%	194	37%	253	37%	359
38%	102	38%	125	38%	155	38%	196	38%	256	38%	363
39%	103	39%	126	39%	156	39%	198	39%	258	39%	366
40%	104	40%	127	40%	158	40%	200	40%	260	40%	369
41%	105	41%	128	41%	159	41%	201	41%	262	41%	372
42%	106	42%	129	42%	160	42%	203	42%	264	42%	375
43%	107	43%	130	43%	161	43%	204	43%	266	43%	377
44%	107	44%	131	44%	162	44%	205	44%	267	44%	379
45%	108	45%	131	45%	163	45%	206	45%	268	45%	381
46%	108	46%	132	46%	163	46%	207	46%	269	46%	382
47%	108	47%	132	47%	164	47%	207	47%	270	47%	383
48%	108	48%	133	48%	164	48%	208	48%	271	48%	384
49%	109	49%	133	49%	164	49%	208	49%	271	49%	385
50%	109	50%	133	50%	164	50%	208	50%	271	50%	385

N = number.

Notes: These sample sizes are based on the Normal Approximation to the Binomial Distribution; a minimum sample size of 30 is required for this approximation to be valid. Shaded areas represent sample sizes of less than 30.

Appendix D-3. Determining Sample Size With a Margin of Error at ± 10 Percent

70% Confidence		75% Confidence		80% Confidence		85% Confidence		90% Confidence		95% Confidence	
Percent Present	N Required	Percent Present	N Required	Percent Present	N Required	Percent Present	N Required	Percent Present	N Required	Percent Present	N Required
1%	2	1%	2	1%	2	1%	3	1%	3	1%	4
2%	3	2%	3	2%	4	2%	5	2%	6	2%	8
3%	4	3%	4	3%	5	3%	7	3%	8	3%	12
4%	5	4%	6	4%	7	4%	8	4%	11	4%	15
5%	6	5%	7	5%	8	5%	10	5%	13	5%	19
6%	7	6%	8	6%	10	6%	12	6%	16	6%	22
7%	8	7%	9	7%	11	7%	14	7%	18	7%	26
8%	8	8%	10	8%	13	8%	16	8%	20	8%	29
9%	9	9%	11	9%	14	9%	17	9%	23	9%	32
10%	10	10%	12	10%	15	10%	19	10%	25	10%	35
11%	11	11%	13	11%	17	11%	21	11%	27	11%	38
12%	12	12%	14	12%	18	12%	22	12%	29	12%	41
13%	13	13%	15	13%	19	13%	24	13%	31	13%	44
14%	14	14%	16	14%	20	14%	25	14%	33	14%	47
15%	14	15%	17	15%	21	15%	27	15%	35	15%	49
16%	15	16%	18	16%	23	16%	28	16%	37	16%	52
17%	16	17%	19	17%	24	17%	30	17%	39	17%	55
18%	16	18%	20	18%	25	18%	31	18%	40	18%	57
19%	17	19%	21	19%	26	19%	32	19%	42	19%	60
20%	18	20%	22	20%	27	20%	34	20%	44	20%	62
21%	18	21%	22	21%	28	21%	35	21%	45	21%	64
22%	19	22%	23	22%	29	22%	36	22%	47	22%	66
23%	20	23%	24	23%	30	23%	37	23%	48	23%	69
24%	20	24%	25	24%	30	24%	38	24%	50	24%	71
25%	21	25%	25	25%	31	25%	39	25%	51	25%	73
26%	21	26%	26	26%	32	26%	40	26%	53	26%	74
27%	22	27%	27	27%	33	27%	41	27%	54	27%	76
28%	22	28%	27	28%	34	28%	42	28%	55	28%	78
29%	23	29%	28	29%	34	29%	43	29%	56	29%	80
30%	23	30%	28	30%	35	30%	44	30%	57	30%	81
31%	24	31%	29	31%	36	31%	45	31%	58	31%	83
32%	24	32%	29	32%	36	32%	46	32%	59	32%	84
33%	24	33%	30	33%	37	33%	46	33%	60	33%	85
34%	25	34%	30	34%	37	34%	47	34%	61	34%	87
35%	25	35%	31	35%	38	35%	48	35%	62	35%	88
36%	25	36%	31	36%	38	36%	48	36%	63	36%	89
37%	26	37%	31	37%	39	37%	49	37%	64	37%	90
38%	26	38%	32	38%	39	38%	49	38%	64	38%	91
39%	26	39%	32	39%	39	39%	50	39%	65	39%	92
40%	26	40%	32	40%	40	40%	50	40%	65	40%	93
41%	27	41%	32	41%	40	41%	51	41%	66	41%	93
42%	27	42%	33	42%	40	42%	51	42%	66	42%	94
43%	27	43%	33	43%	41	43%	51	43%	67	43%	95
44%	27	44%	33	44%	41	44%	52	44%	67	44%	95
45%	27	45%	33	45%	41	45%	52	45%	67	45%	96
46%	27	46%	33	46%	41	46%	52	46%	68	46%	96
47%	27	47%	33	47%	41	47%	52	47%	68	47%	96
48%	27	48%	34	48%	41	48%	52	48%	68	48%	96
49%	28	49%	34	49%	41	49%	52	49%	68	49%	97
50%	28	50%	34	50%	41	50%	52	50%	68	50%	97

N = number.

Notes: These sample sizes are based on the Normal Approximation to the Binomial Distribution; a minimum sample size of 30 is required for this approximation to be valid. Shaded areas represent sample sizes of less than 30.

Appendix E. Example of a Form Used To Document Past Soil Disturbance in an Activity Area

Documentation of Soil Disturbance

Date: _____

Project Name: _____

Stand or Unit ID: _____

Observer(s): _____

Name of Old Timber Sale (if known): _____

Lat./Long. and Datum: _____

        ❏   **No past disturbance visible**

Check all that apply

Type	Past Disturbance	Approximate Age/Timber Sale Name
Stumps*		
– with disturbance nearby		
– without obvious disturbance		
Skid Trails		
Excavated Skid Trails		
Old Roads		
– decommissioned		
– storage		
Skyline Corridors		
Landings		
Slash Piles		
Horse Logging		
Homestead/Pasture		
Other		

Stumps could be from ground-based, skyline, helicopter logging, or firewood cutting.

Comments:

Appendix F. Technical Specifications of Portable Data Recorders

Portable data recorders (PDRs) come in many varieties. It is possible, and not uncommon, to see scientists in the field carrying laptop computers, some with attached instruments that transmit data directly into a spreadsheet or database form. Many smaller devices provide almost the same capabilities, with the exception that data transfer occurs only when the device is connected to a computer after the user returns to the office. The type of PDR a user carries into the field depends partly on personal preference, partly on the capability of the device, and partly on what is available for purchase. Forest Service users generally are limited to what is listed on the corporate contract. Contracts change as new technology becomes available, so rushing to purchase one type of PDR may preclude acquiring another type better suited to the task.

In general, if the user is going to be constantly in motion or changing locations at regular or relatively short intervals, the device should be comparatively small, lightweight, and conveniently accessible. The device must be capable of running whatever software is used for the data recording and processing needs and must have sufficient storage capacity. An optional capability is wireless connectivity for immediate data transfer.

For the Forest Soil Disturbance Monitoring Protocol and use of the electronic field form, the requirements are as follows:

- Microsoft operating system (Pocket PC, Windows CE, etc.) or other operating system that can run compatible spreadsheet software.
- Pocket Excel (or Excel Mobile) or other compatible spreadsheet software.
- Screen that is visible in direct sunlight and under a thick forest canopy.
- Touchscreen or keypad data input.
- Connectivity for data download and upload.

The following specifications are highly recommended:

- Small (handheld or tablet).
- Lightweight, to allow for several hours of carriage at a time.
- Rugged and weatherproof, or with a padded and weatherproof case.
- Battery life of at least 8 hours.
- Serial and/or USB connectors.
- Minimum of 32MB of memory.

The following accessories are recommended:

- Additional storage capacity (e.g., compact flash cards).
- Rechargeable or spare batteries.
- In-car charger.

The following features are optional:

- Network or wireless connectivity.
- Global Positioning System (GPS) card.
- Geographic Information System (GIS) display software.
- Carrying case.
- Bring laptop along (keep in car or at lodging) for nightly data transfer to ensure against data loss.
- If your PDR is not rugged or weatherproof, bring zipping-style bags and a lanyard to tie the recorder to yourself.

One choice is the Trimble or TDS Recon Pocket PC handheld field data collector ($1,799 and up). Immersible and shock resistant, it runs Microsoft Windows Mobile 2003 software, which includes Pocket Excel and Pocket Word. It has an illuminated color touch-screen display (2 ¼" x 3 7/8") with software, keyboard, and 64MB of active memory. The Recon Pocket PC can, in most cases, store an entire day's data collection. The Recon also provides 64MB of flash memory for backups. If more storage is needed, two covered CF adapters are available for expanded memory. These can also accommodate add-ons such as GPS or a modem. The Recon Pocket PC runs GIS software called "SOLO" or "ARCPAD" that can help locate you in the field, including using background images, shapefile-format activity area polygons, and GPS location.

The Recon uses a "PowerBoot Module" instead of standard rechargeable batteries. The PowerBoot Module, when fully charged, typically provides approximately 15 hours of battery life. An AC adapter/charger is included in the base price.

If you choose this option, we recommend the 400Mhz version, with 64MB of RAM and 128MB of flash memory, to eliminate the need for additional cards. We also bought the optional in-car charger and extra data transfer cables. (We lost one almost immediately.) Our crews were able to remain in the field for extended periods, unconcerned about power loss or data storage limitations.

Another, less expensive, choice is a Compaq (now HP) Ipaq 3600, which also runs the Pocket PC software. It has 32MB of memory, which is divided between "storage" memory and "program" memory. Capacity can be expanded if you also purchase a hard sleeve, which incorporates a compact flash card slot. This product, however, is neither weatherproof nor shock resistant. Prices start at $499.99. Accessories such as in-car adapters are available.

Drawbacks of these handheld recorders include a small viewing area—an important limitation due to the size of the input form used with the visual indicators. Also, input speed (response time of the mobile software to stylus taps) and the dexterity required for precise stylus tapping are factors that affect the efficiency of the exercise. A ruggedized upgrade of the Husky FeX21 is available; it runs Microsoft's Handheld PC 2000 operating system, has a builtin keyboard, and is priced at $1,999.

Tablet-style recorders, with the ability to display an 8.5" x 11" page, are perhaps a better choice, providing a view of more of the data input spreadsheet. Prices range from ~$850.00 to more than $2,000.00, depending on brand name and configuration. If you are able to purchase this option (there are two on the Forest Service contract as of May 2009), remember that the response time is dependent on processor speed and RAM. Look for outdoor visibility, battery life, and ruggedness.

Other handheld computers may be comparable. Any unit that meets the requirements listed previously can be used. There may be compatible equipment that has fallen out of use in your local organization and can be borrowed or bartered. Husky Brand field data recorders were in vogue not long ago for use in cruising timber, etc. They are suited for the work presented in this guide, because they satisfy the operating system and software requirements, although they must be protected from the weather and handled with care. Check with local timber management personnel and others for availability.

A nontechnical alternative is to use paper forms in the field and transfer the data to the electronic spreadsheet upon return to the office or temporary duty station. One advantage to this method is that the drop-down lists useful on the PC version of the spreadsheet do not function after transfer to handheld, field-going PDRs—a consequence of the limited instruction set available in the mobile operating system. The lack of some sort of computer in the field, however, will require the user to rely on tables or hand calculations of the minimum required sample size and the statistical results of the monitoring activity.

Appendix G. Core Site Descriptors for Each Activity Area

This information is placed on form 1 of the FSDMPSoLo spreadsheet.

A separate report must be filed for each unit (or subunit) in a project. Definitions are provided in appendix D. To the extent possible, each report must include the following information:

- Project ID: Usually a name, such as "Quarling Eagles" or "Marty Sale."
  Unit ID: Most often a number; could be alphanumeric, such as "12A."
  Project Type: For example, "Green sale," "Salvage sale," "Fuels Abatement."

- Location
  Region: Name, rather than number, to avoid cumbersome lookup.
  Forest: Name, rather than number, to avoid cumbersome lookup.
  District: Name, rather than number, to avoid cumbersome lookup.

- Map Information
  USGS Quad(s): Name(s) of 7.5-minute quadrangle map(s) of site.
  Geographic Coordinates: Either latitude & longitude (preferred) or UTM.

- Topography
  Landform Description/Category: Such as "Glaciated hillslope" or "Alluvial terrace."
  Slope: In percent, the average or range of steepness of the unit or subunit.
  Aspect: In degrees, the prevalent or range of direction the unit faces.
  Elevation: In feet, the average or range of elevation of the unit or subunit.

- Ecology
  Ecological Subsection: The alphanumeric subsection ID where the unit appears.
  Habitat Type: The vegetative community classification of the unit.
  Watershed ID: The name and the 6th-level HUC of the watershed containing the unit.
  Watershed Condition Class: I, II, or III (defined in FSM 2521.1).

- Landtype Association: The mapping unit ID, based on landtype grouping.
  Parent Material: Source material of the predominant soil on the site.
  Soil Classification: The taxonomic descriptor of the predominant soil.
  Soil Survey: Name of the published/accepted survey of the site area.

- Site History

  Fire Activity: Season and year of historic fire(s).

  Harvest Activity: Season and year of previous harvest(s).

  Grazing Activity: Span of years of allotted grazing.

  Site Prep: Season and year and type of site prep work.

  Planting: Year of planting, species planted, stocking rate.

  Thinning: Year of thinning, residual stocking rate, species mix.

  Reclamation: Of roads, landings, or other disturbance, the year(s).

  Recreational Use: Type and duration of recreation activities.

- Current Activity

  Prescription: Based on residual stocking rate, or "clearcut," "dispersed shelterwood," etc.

  Logging System: Type of equipment used in current activity.

  Monitoring Type: Number of months preactivity or postactivity.

  Soil Moisture: Measured at time of monitoring.

- Summary Statistics: These will be filled automatically as transect is assessed.

- Administrative Information: Most of this information is filled automatically.

  Observer Name:

  Observer Title:

  Date Monitored:

  Date of Report:

  Date Approved: {All reports must be approved by next-level line officer before final submission.}

  Approver Name:

  Approver Title:

  NEPA Document: Title of NEPA document associated with this project.

  Date NEPA Completed: